MARILYN LAWRENCE

the
Anorexic
Experience

THIRD EDITION
FULLY REVISED AND UPDATED

THIS EDITION EDITED

BY KATE MOSSE

First published by The Women's Press Ltd, 1984
A member of the Namara Group
34 Great Sutton Street, London EC1V 0DX

Reprinted 1984, 1985
Reprinted and revised 1988, 1995
Reprinted 1998

British Library Cataloguing-in-Publication Data
Lawrence, Marilyn
    The Anorexic Experience. – (Women's Press handbook series; 3)
    1. Anorexic nervosa
    I. Title
    616.85'2   RC552.A.5

ISBN 0 7043 4441 6

Typeset in Times by Contour Typesetters, Southall, London
Printed and bound in Great Britain by
Cox & Wyman Ltd, Reading, Berks

For Joseph

Contents

Preface to the Third Edition

I am grateful to The Women's Press for giving me the opportunity to look again at *The Anorexic Experience*, ten years after its original publication. I have decided to make only minor changes and additions to update the text, leaving the book substantially unaltered.

It has been an interesting and rather difficult experience for me to go back to the book again after so long. It has made me realise how much has changed since I wrote it, but also in other ways, how little. Certainly I have changed and if I wrote *The Anorexic Experience* now, it would be a very different kind of book. I do not necessarily think it would be a better book though. Although I am now more interested in the inner, unconscious world of the anorexic and the dynamics of the therapeutic relationship than I was then, I am pleased to find that I remain committed to the perspective developed here. I am delighted to learn that health care professionals as well as sufferers and their families continue to find the book useful.

One of the most significant developments in recent years has been the recognition of the prevalence of bulimia, (an eating disorder characterised by over-eating, often followed by self-induced vomiting or laxative use.) Those of us who were working in this field in the 1970s knew that some women suffered from this rather different problem with food. We did not have a name for it and I think we were all rather reluctant to take it seriously. Unlike anorexia, bulimia is a secret symptom; it does not show and the woman is able to carry on with her life as though nothing is wrong. Bulimia is a symptom which has attracted even less understanding and sympathy than anorexia. Troy Cooper's chapter in *Fed up and Hungry*[1] documents the way in which health professionals and researchers have reacted to bulimic women as if they are failed anorexics, utterly lacking in self-control and without the anorexics' mysterious iron will and determined self-denial. Recently, the Princess of Wales, a very popular figure in the UK, 'confessed' to being bulimic. It will be interesting to see if this does anything to change public attitudes to the problem. My fear is that it may ultimately contribute to a loss of sympathy for the Princess.

Although there are many links between anorexia and bulimia, and in spite of the fact that some women will suffer from both during the course of their lives, I do believe that they are better understood as separate conditions. The underlying problems may be similar, or even identical, but the experiences, both of the sufferer and of those who try to help are very different. With this in mind, I published in 1988, with my friend and colleague Mira Dana, *Women's Secret Disorder: A New Understanding of Bulimia*. This book takes up and develops many of the themes first articulated in *The Anorexic Experience*. However, I think the reader would agree with me that the mood and atmosphere of the two books is very different. *The Anorexic Experience* is concerned to describe and reveal the coldness, the deadness, the utter self-annihilation which feels for the anorexic the only way to survive. The bulimic woman, on the other hand, actually experiences her aggression, destructiveness, her murderous greed. But in a split-off, encapsulated way, a way which makes her feel terrified and guilty. The anorexic woman keeps her guilt always at bay; if she does not eat, she has nothing for which to reproach herself. The two conditions are really mirror images of each other, representing very different but linked states of mind. While this book will certainly be of interest to sufferers of bulimia and to those wanting to understand them, it was, specifically, the experience of the anorexic which I sought to capture and convey.

The last decade has of course seen the dramatic deterioration of the National Health Service, with mental health services suffering crippling cutbacks. While the closure of the large mental hospitals is to be welcomed on grounds of good practice, the policy of simply with-drawing services from ill people has been a catastrophe. When I wrote *The Anorexic Experience*, I was critical of the kind of treatment anorexics were often offered. In the present situation I am angry to have to say that they are sometimes not offered any treatment at all. There has been an increase in the number of units specialising in the treatment of eating disorders and this has meant that, at least for some patients, services have been somewhat protected. However, in many areas of the country, specialist services do not exist and people suffering with anorexia simply take their place in the ever-lengthening queue for treatment. In a climate which emphasises cost-effectiveness and where cheap, fast treatments are sought, long-term psychotherapy can seem like an expensive luxury. I have seen two cases this year of young anorexic women discharged after lengthy admissions to mental hospitals where out-patient follow-up treatment was not offered. Both were simply given appointments to see a dietician! Whatever else we may know or not know about anorexia, we know it cannot be cured by dietary advice. Both of these young women were subsequently re-admitted to hospital, which highlights the fact that on economic grounds alone, the failure actually to understand and resolve an anorexic episode is disastrous. It is of course also a human tragedy for the young women concerned and for their families. In a Health Service starved of cash, in which units operate in an independent way, often in competition with each other, seeming to stagger from one financial crisis to the next, it is very difficult to commit the modest but long-term resources required to treat an anorexic with out-patient psychotherapy.

In spite of the chronic shortage of psychotherapy in the National Health Service, there is, I think, an increasing acknowledgement among clinicians that psychotherapy is both necessary and potentially effective for people with eating disorders. While hospitalisation for refeeding remains a common treatment, few would now claim that on its own it is likely to be effective. For all my anxiety and pessimism about the state of the National Health Service and its capacity to provide even a reasonable service for people with eating disorders, I remain very impresssed indeed by the many creative and devoted professionals who continue to struggle to offer the very best they can to their patients and clients.

The last ten years has also seen the increasing erosion of the stereotype of the anorexic as a middle-class, white teenager. While there does seem to be a link between anorexia and high educational achievement (which I explore further in *Fed Up and Hungry*[2]) it is now clear that anorexia is no respecter of race, age or social class. In a recent article on early onset anorexia, Bryan Lask and Rachel Bryant Waugh[3] conclude that anorexia in children as young as eight is probably on the increase. This suggests that at earlier and earlier ages, girls are using their bodies as a focus for their unhappiness. The one statistic which shows no sign of changing is the ratio of female to male sufferers; ten years age 10 to 1 was the usual figure given and most clinicians would still feel that to be about right today. We still have no authoritative 'answer' to the question of why anorexia is such an overwhelmingly female disorder and I believe *The Anorexic Experience* continues to make a contribution to that discussion.

Since 1985, clinicians have begun to notice a link between eating disorders (anorexia and bulimia) and reported sexual abuse.[4] This was an important finding, and it is not difficult to understand how the need to take control of the body might assume such importance for women who have been subject to abuse. There are, however, dangers in assuming that there is a clear cause-and-effect relationship between sexual abuse and eating disorders. We know that sexual abuse in childhood can have far-reaching, damaging effects on the whole personality and the capacity to form relationships. We know for example, that it is not only women with eating disorders who quite frequently have a history of sexual abuse, but women (and men) who suffer from a variety of other mental illnesses as well. We must also bear in mind that many anorexics do not have such a history. There can be few more distressing experiences for a patient and her family than for clinicians to assume that because she has anorexia, she must have been sexually abused. We need to continue to try to understand the experience of the anorexic – her past and her present experience. This may lead us beyond simple physical abuse to the more subtle and unconscious wrongs we do one another as well as to the particular sensitivities of children who eventually become anorexic. Much work remains to be done. Perhaps this is the agenda for the next decade.

London 1994

Acknowledgements

My sincere thanks are due to the following people.

In the early days, to those who encouraged me to take my strange preoccupation seriously: John Lawrence, Denis Sharp, German Berrios.

To Janice, who taught me almost all I know.

Later, to Hilary Rose, Helen Roberts, Sheila Allen and other friends at the University of Bradford.

Then to Gill Edwards, Jane Almond and everyone who had to do with Anorexia Counselling Service.

To Celia Lowenstein.

More recently, to all friends and colleagues at the Women's Therapy Centre, but especially to Mira Dana.

To David Whitehouse, whose interest in my work has been much appreciated.

To Will Pennycook, who has done more for this book than to provide its conclusion.

To Ros de Lanerolle, who has taught me that it is possible to be both sisterly and business-like.

To Geoffrey Pearson.

To Carol and baby Matthew; they made the book easier to finish.

And to all clients, past and present.

We would like to acknowledge the permission of Michael B. Yeats and Macmillan London Ltd for the use of the poem *For Anne Gregory* by W. B. Yeats; Virago Press for quotations from *The Art of Starvation* by Sheila MacLeod, Virago, 1981; and Frederick Muller Ltd for quotations from *How to Survive Anorexia* by Peter Lambley, 1983.

Introduction

This book aims primarily to be of help to women who are, or who think they might be, suffering from anorexia. It should make it easier for you to understand what is happening to you, and to see that your difficulties are not necessarily the result of your own individual circumstances only, but a reflection of problems encountered by very many women in our society. It should also help you to decide what kind of help or treatment you need, and how you might go about finding it.

I am well aware that parents, teachers, counsellors and many other members of the 'helping professions' often find anorexia a particularly difficult set of symptoms to understand and to work with. The second aim of this book is to help them to achieve a better understanding of the issues involved and to feel more confident about having something to offer to the women who come to them for help.

In spite of a vast and growing literature on anorexia, there are certain very intriguing and fundamental questions which up until now have remained unexplored. Why are the vast majority of people who suffer from anorexia women? Why do middle-class (or more accurately, educated) women appear to be more vulnerable? Why does it seem to be a problem of the affluent West, the developed and well-fed parts of the world? And why is it increasing?

In attempting to find some answers to these questions, it becomes clear that if we regard anorexia as a form of 'mental illness' which afflicts some unfortunate individuals, we will fail to take account of it as a problem for women which has its origins and roots in the societies in which it exists.

We need to remember also that very many women who would not

usually be classified as 'anorexic' actually have profound and painful difficulties in the area of food and eating, and in the way they think about their bodies. Indeed, it is probably true to say that in a society which has such ambivalent and contradictory attitudes to women and to womanliness, most women will at some time in our lives experience difficulties in this direction.

We can then begin to understand anorexia as an extension of the difficulties which women have with and around our weight and the food we eat; it no longer appears as something 'different', outside the range or ordinary experience. It is in fact at one end of a continuum of confused and conflicted responses which as we women have towards ourselves. The third aim of this book then, is to offer some account of the development of young women, of their position in this society and to examine why some of them experience an anorexic episode, while others do not.

The label 'anorexic' is often used in unhelpful ways. When a woman is said to be 'an anorexic', it sounds as though a permanent state of being is being described; rather as if she had taken on a different identity. This kind of description tends to colour our thinking about the whole problem. It might be more helpful to think of such a woman as a woman who, at a particular stage in her development, can find no other means of expressing how she feels about herself and other people. If you believe yourself to 'be anorexic', it is particularly important that you try to see this as a stage or a phrase in your life – and one which you need not get stuck in.

A number of attempts have been made in recent years to categorise or classify different forms and types of anorexia.

For instance, the form of eating disorder which has been called 'bulimia' is often separated out from other difficulties with food. 'Bulimic' is a term which is usually used to describe women who eat, but then make themselves sick. Women with this symptom are very preoccupied with food and with avoiding weight gain, so vomiting is used as a means of maintaining a low weight while eating quite large amounts of food. Much of what follows will apply to you if you have this kind of eating disorder as well as to those of you who stay thin by avoiding food.

Throughout the book, I refer to anorexia as though it is always a problem which effects women. This, I know, is not the case. There are a considerable and possibly growing number of anorexic men. Those men I have worked with many justifiably wonder why I appear to have forgotten them. I haven't. But my concern here has been to analyse who so many 'anorexics' are women, rather than why a few of them are men. Anorexia is a problem crucially related to women's psychology, which is in turn related to women's way of being in the world. The fact that it also sometimes effects men only indicates that the psychology of women and men is not wholly distinct: issues which are problematic for most women can also be so for some men.

Finally, I usually use the term 'anorexia' and 'bulimia' rather than 'anorexia nervosa' and 'bulimia nervosa'. I do this for simplicity.

1
Beyond Understanding

Anorexia Nervosa is a most puzzling and perplexing phenomenon to try to understand. If you are a woman in the midst of an anorexic phase, you are probably as confused by what is happening to you as everybody else is. Even those of you who have recovered from anorexia and have left it far behind might still find it hard to give an account of what it is all about.

To women who have not experienced anorexia themselves, the whole thing might at first appear to be quite outside their range of understanding. There is a temptation to try to make sense of anorexia as though it were an illness, totally alien to the experience of 'normal' women. Those women who are or have been anorexic will know how frightening and alienating it feels to try to explain to another woman how you feel, only to be met with blank incomprehension, or worse, to be treated as though you are mad. And yet it is only when we begin to approach the problem as an extension of the difficulties which all women have in our lives, that we can really begin to make sense of the experience itself, and of the issues which underlie it.

Since many people who work with anorexic women have not themselves had the experience of anorexia, for them, understanding presents its own special problems. I say this with some conviction, for I have spent a good number of years trying to understand. To some extent this book stands as a record of my attempts.

I first met a woman in an acutely anorexic phase something approaching a decade ago. I can remember the occasion well although I had no means of knowing at the time that this was an important landmark in my professional life.

I was a psychiatric social worker, she an in-patient in the unit in which I worked. I hadn't long been qualified and my training had encouraged me to interpret my role as being in some way 'different' from, 'other' than the 'patients' with whom I worked. Indeed, most of the clients with whom I worked were very different from me. I had all the advantages in life while they had very few. Their symptoms were the expressions of the bad deals, either materially or emotionally, which life sometimes hands out. As far as understanding went, it was not usually hard to see why they sat where they sat and why I sat where I did.

Then Sandra came into my office and into my world. I had seen her before in ward meetings and found her something of an enigma there. She was not a 'difficult' patient (yet). On the contrary, she was clearly very caring and perceptive. A rather lovely young woman who hid her natural charm to some extent under a kind of mousiness. Apart from being thin, she looked quite ordinary.

I knew about anorexia of course. When I was at school, some girls I did not know 'got it'. People said it was the influence of Twiggy. Today perhaps Kate Moss would be held responsible. The girls left hurriedly and I always thought they must really have wanted to be fashion models. Sandra seemed rather a serious person and did not look at all as though she wanted to be one . . .

She came in and we chatted for a while. Quite a long while, I suspect. How old was she? Just a few years younger than myself, as it turned out. In terms of her recent past, it transpired that she had graduated from a neighbouring university to my own in a similar combination of subjects. We talked about poetry a bit, and about painting. She really got me thinking about Van Gogh. She was in fact a very engaging person and, for once, it was not too clear to me why she was 'the patient'.

She had gone to university with mixed feelings. Her family had its problems and when she had left them, she was feeling rather guilty about pursuing her own self-development and leaving them to manage without her. I could understand that. I did not say much about myself, then or ever I think, but it was quite clear to me at the time that I was *identifying* with Sandra and that I was quickly getting to like her.

I thought I ought to begin to explore the issue which had brought us together. I invited her to tell me about the difficulties she had with food and her weight. The change in her manner was dramatic. She looked frightened, talked fast. She did not know why she felt as she did, but the feelings were more powerful than anything she had ever felt before. Food was obviously utterly terrifying. She still felt, at her pitifully low weight, that she was too fat. She could acknowledge that she was 'wrong' and that quite probably she ought to gain some weight, yet the thought was repulsive to her. This, I thought, is madness. Yet it was not a mad woman I was speaking to. Until five minutes ago, before we got on to the subject of weight, I had thought of Sandra as the kind of person I would probably enjoy talking to at a party. Now this other, incomprehensible Sandra. I could not believe it. People had told me that 'anorexics' were really quite unreasonable. But she was not, except about her body and the way she nourished it.

In this short and superficial account of what must have been a rather short and superficial interview is contained the rationale for much of what subsequently took place, not only between Sandra and myself, but in my increasing interest in the problem of anorexia.

Gradually I began to learn more about Sandra. I began to see her as someone who found life difficult in a more general way than I had realised. What struck me in particular was her huge and immovable sense of guilt. She thought of herself as mean and selfish, which she certainly was not. Anything she did, unless it entailed ultimate self sacrifices, would be evidence of her utter uselessness. She experienced herself as a parasite, a worthless thing with nothing to give to anyone. My protestations to the contrary were of no use at all. She heard me talking of grace, but she knew she was not among the chosen. Yet she continued to cover this profound sense of worthlessness with a weary and sometimes even cheerful commitment to doing the right thing, to getting better and to finding a means of being 'useful'.

The problem for me was that I could find nothing within myself which would help me to understand what Sandra was saying to me.

The first breakthrough in my understanding came when I was trying (so far in vain) to relate her difficulties about food and eating to her rather over-developed moral sense. Overcome with frustration and with wanting her to begin to see herself as I saw her, I found myself raising my voice and squeaking, 'But eating's not a moral issue!' (If I'd had a table to hand, I would probably have thumped on it.)

She looked at me, slightly amused, somewhat superior, and said, 'Well – it is.'

I do not know what happened next, but I could not forget what she had said. She was right, of course, *it is*!

I began to understand from my own experience what it was she had meant. Greed and self-indulgence, our own or other people's, offends us in a moral way. Think of the feeling after Christmas when everyone has spent three or four days (or more if we are lucky) engaging in persistent self-indulgence. We feel spoiled by our own greed; spoiled not just in a physical sense, which may or may not be important to us, but spoiled in a moral sense too. Our immediate response is to take up running, to go and play a few games of squash to 'work it off'. This reaction is not simply a remedy for our bodies, but the physical hardship and endurance applies salve to the soul as well. We behave as though the body is indeed the mirror of the soul. Fat people, simply by virtue of their shape and size, seem to be telling us that they are careless, indolent, lacking in self-control and even in sensitivity. We know this is not true, but we behave as though it is. Sandra, by cruelly manipulating her body into the perfect ideal of thinness, was trying to say all the opposite things about herself. I had discovered that she was an ascetic. And more importantly, that these were feelings which I and other people were able to understand.

My experiences with Sandra also made me think about the attitudes of so-called 'normal' women to food and to our bodies. I began to realise that the behaviour of most of us is, in a real sense, quite strange. Most of us are not regarded as having illnesses, and yet to call our attitudes to food, to eating and to our bodies 'normal' is to make an unusual use of the word. We do not just eat: we slim, we worry, we weight watch. We also spend an inordinate amount of time absorbed in the business of food: feeding others as well or instead of ourselves, shopping, cooking and clearing up the waste. The chapter which follows is an attempt to clarify my thinking about this, to try to get beyond the idea that anorexia is simply slimming gone mad, and to document the disordered set of relationships which women have with and around food.

By this time, I had started to read books about anorexia. Most of them left me more confused than I had been before. I was starting to get a steady trickle of new referrals of anorexic women. The books did not seem to answer any of the questions I was beginning to formulate. The women I was meeting were all interesting, thoughtful and intelligent. Why should this particular group of women, suddenly, out of the blue, as it always seemed, develop such a deadly preoccupation with their bodies and their weight? What was happening to these women which did not happen to others, which gave them such a precarious sense of who they were? Surely all women are subject to the same social pressures to be slim and to have bodies which people approve of? Why did some of the brightest and best of us need to express distress in such dramatic and self-defeating ways?

Feminist literature at the time seemed to concentrate on women's failures. The focus seemed to be on why women did not do well in education, why we failed to achieve. And yet so many of the women I was meeting had done or were doing very well at school and were successful in their own right. Chapter 3 represents my attempts to discover the answers to some of these questions.

Meanwhile, Sandra continued not to get better. She was discharged, readmitted and discharged again. She lived on a knife edge. She did not know how to eat and she did not know how to live. She described her feelings about food as 'like being in a state of continual civil war'. It always seemed to me that she was in a state of siege, but unlike most besieged people, the armies which surrounded her were attempting to feed rather than to starve her.

At about that time, I met Janet, a woman in her early 30s. She described to me one day how she would spend her lunch hours walking from one cake shop to another, looking in the windows, smelling the newly baked bread, thinking about the possibilities of going in and buying something, but never venturing over the threshold. That image of the starving woman, confronted with abundance, but unable to nourish herself at all, impressed me deeply. I did not know how to understand it, but I could not forget it. I have since discovered it to be a very familiar story and one which many women will recognise.

Then there was Sarah. She would sit in sleeveless clothes by an open window in mid-winter until she went blue. I myself hate being cold almost more than anything else and I remember feeling so sorry that someone felt they had to endure it, day after miserable day. Yet Sarah was striving to overcome her human nature, which she felt to be weakness. I have since learnt to recognise this too as a compulsion which many women share.

Gradually it began to dawn on me that these women seemed to endure, even seek out physical sensations like cold and hunger simply so that they could overcome them. The important thing was the sense of power and control which this overcoming brought with it. The frame began to widen. If the need to subdue and take control of the body was so great, then surely an underlying issue must be a sense of lack of control in other areas of life.

Here again it was possible to understand the life difficulties of women with anorexia in exactly the same ways as we can understand the difficulties which all women encounter in our lives.

Anorexia affects a very fundamental area of all human experience and concern: the relationship between ourselves and our bodies, between us and what we eat. And other people's reactions to anorexia seem to confirm the idea that it touches on themes common to us all. Most people are very *interested* in it. A common reaction among women when it is mentioned is: 'I wish I could catch it for a while' or 'I could do with a dose of that'. This indicates, I think, that many women are aware that the area of their lives concerning food and their own size and shape is not altogether a happy one.

Normal understanding and being misunderstood

On the other hand, the behaviour associated with anorexia does seem to most people very strange and bizarre. It seems to be the kind of craziness that we can at best sympathise with, but never come anywhere near identifying with. And in some ways, this reaction is a legitimate one: these are not normal experiences, and most people will never come to know them at first hand. It is small wonder that a woman in an anorexic phase frequently feels misunderstood. She probably is misunderstood.

So to say that anorexia defies logical understanding is almost certainly true. But it becomes simpler to understand when we recognise that many other people's 'normal' feelings about eating and food, our bodies and our weight, are not particularly logical aspects of our own experience either.

How many of us, I wonder, when life begins to get us down a bit – work is too difficult, our personal lives are not as well ordered as we would like – look at ourselves in the mirror and conclude that if only we could lose half a stone everything would be much better? Logically, the only thing that would happen is that our clothes would not fit. And yet the temptation to try to solve real problems by changing our physical selves is one which most women have probably encountered in themselves. Sometimes we are tempted to live in the future as far as our size and weight are concerned. It is not uncommon for women to buy clothes a size too small, telling themselves, 'I will shrink into it – that will be the incentive I need to lose that half stone.' Perhaps we sometimes accept invitations or plan holidays believing that by the time they come about, we shall be wearing a size 12 instead of a size 14. Some of us may manage to bring about the prophecy that we have set up; most of us probably do not and end up wearing the new dress or the bikini and wishing we had bought a size larger.

You will probably fail to understand your own experience if you persist in thinking of it as a kind of illness, as though the 'symptoms' have descended from another planet. On the contrary, we must understand it as a disorder which springs from the very midst of women's experience of the world.

It now becomes possible to recognise that anorexia is not the problem, but the solution. It is the solution to a problem which at the time we find impossible to deal with in any other way. If we can understand it in this way, we can see why it is so painfully difficult to give anorexia up.

While it is right to understand an anorexic episode as a cry for help, to recognise it as a sign that a woman needs to find a different kind of solution, it is also in a real sense a 'No Entry' sign.

Those of you who have had some experience of anorexia will know how very safe it feels to live within and behind the walls of your solution. The feeling that your anorexia protects you is a perfectly legitimate one. It does. Although it might at times be a terribly painful and distressing state of mind and body, it feels as though *you* are safe inside.

One way of understanding this sense of safety which anorexia offers is use of the idea of the true and the false self.[1] By 'false self', I do not mean something which is phoney or artificial or dishonest. Rather, the false self needs to be understood as a positive attempt to protect the true self, which feels threatened and vulnerable.

There is nothing wrong with needing something to shelter behind. If we were to expose our true selves to the world *all the time*, we should all be too vulnerable to find life bearable at all. So all of us, in some degree, must develop a false self which can absorb some of the blows.

For some individuals, the false self may be no more than a capacity to be polite and compliant under certain circumstances: to maintain a comfortable social manner, for instance, which is not directly related to what is actually happening inside. Others of us develop a false self in relation to our jobs, protecting the precious and vulnerable parts of ourselves by presenting a competent and resilient front. We have what our friends refer to as a 'telephone voice', which we drop as soon as we realise it is a friend at the other end of the line.

In a similar way, we can think of the symptoms of anorexia as a kind of protective outer shell. The shell is not the real person, but it hides and protects the real person. The important point is that the real self is still there, underneath.

Often, women who are in the midst of an anorexic episode feel as though there is nothing else to them than the defensive structure of their symptoms. Stella, a 22-year-old teacher, said at an initial counselling session, 'You know I sometimes think I'm really dead. It's as though my body just hasn't noticed. Inside, I am dead. I don't have any feelings about anything which matters. I don't really even have any thoughts of my own. I think about food – well, it seems like *all* the time. I wish I didn't, but the thoughts just come and I can't get rid of them. It really is an obsession.'

What Stella was describing was really her way of coping. She had managed to hide her true self to the extent that she could not even experience its existence. But what had she hidden it with? And what was the anorexia saying? Using her anorexia, she had created an outer shell which was strong and invulnerable. It did not need love, it did not need friendship, it did not need food. It had no connection with anyone or anything in its environment. It was complete and contained within itself. It had declared its independence.

If we understand Stella's experience as a way of coping, as an attempt to protect her true self, then we might expect to find beneath her superself all the very qualities which her anorexia denies. It is her vulnerable self, her dependent self, with all the needs of an unhappy little girl. By the time Stella began to talk about herself, she had become very depressed by the pointlessness of her rigid and lonely existence. But still the idea of giving up the solution was too terrifying to contemplate.

Stella describes her preoccupation with food as an obsession. Many of you would probably describe your own difficulties in the same way. Having an 'obsession' really amounts to losing control of how much you think about something, how much energy you devote to it and how seriously you take it. It is impossible to ignore the thoughts, because to do so makes you too anxious. If you try to ignore the thoughts or to resist the compulsive actions which they drive you to, you experience enormous internal conflict the pressure of which can only be relieved by falling back on the rituals and giving in to the obsessive thoughts.

Obsessive thoughts tend to follow when we are faced with conflict which we cannot find any way of resolving. The original source of the conflict, the contradictory feelings inside us, become lost and repressed. The obsession, painful and difficult though it may be in its own right, enables us to remain unaware of the real nature of our conflicting needs. Sometimes the nature of the obsession itself can give us some clues about the conflict which it conceals. In the case of the anorexic obsession with food, the conflict seems to be about nurturance: about being given good things and about giving ourselves good things. To experience a desperate need for nourishment but at the same time a real compulsion to avoid it might lead us to wonder whether the original conflict which the 'obsession' obscures lies in the area of dependence versus independence, the need to be looked after against the need to cope alone. The obsessional aspect of anorexia is without doubt a desperate need to be in control – and yet you will often experience it as an overwhelming feeling that loss of control is just around the next corner.

One of the central difficulties about the set of symptoms we call anorexia is that they really do their job properly. So while I can describe anorexia as a complex set of defences which protect the woman inside from a variety of hurtful conflicts in her life, you will not necessarily experience your difficulties in that way at all. Sheila MacLeod[2] describes these difficulties when she looks back on her own anorexic episode as a teenager: she describes the surface meanings and the hidden meanings of anorexia as a text and a sub-text, the latter being denied both by Sheila herself and by those around her.

'The anorexic's skinny body proclaims, "I have won; I am someone now," ' she writes. 'But thinness, as opposed to slimness, also carries connotations of weightlessness and emptiness. The sub-text to be read in that skinny body is, "I am weightless/worthless; I am empty/nobody. This is what my behaviour is all about." The strategy works by means of a paradox, a paradox which has ultimately to be resolved through some sort of fusion between the apparent text and the sub-text. But in the first, euphoric phase of the disease, only the apparent text is granted recognition by the anorexic.'

Later she says, 'I had discovered an area of my life over which others had no control. And although the sub-text of my increasing thinness (which I chose to ignore) read, "I am doing this because I feel so helpless that not even my own body belongs to me", the apparent text read to me and increasingly to others, "My body is my own and I can do what I like with it".'

The important point here is that it was only in retrospect that Sheila was able to read the sub-text, to understand the underlying meaning of what was happening to her.

If it were true that a woman in an anorexic phase could never have the slightest idea that her anorexia concealed her vulnerable self, that the text has a sub-text, then there is no way that what I have to say here can be of any help to any of you who find yourselves in that position. Fortunately, though, nothing is clearly defined. While you may need the protection of your anorexia to shelter you from some of the painful implications of your own particular conflicts – and in the short term I believe 'need' is the right word – you may still at times be able to be aware that there is more to you than meets the eye!

Acknowledging that we have needs is always a painful and frightening step to take; it is much safer to deny them and to strive to be strong and self-sufficient. During an anorexic phase you may have succeeded in denying your needs to the extent that you do not actually know what they are any more; you may be quite 'out of touch' with certain aspects of yourself. The process of recovery then becomes one of rediscovering yourself.

The approach suggested here is one which encourages you to move at your own pace, to appreciate and rediscover what lies behind your own anorexia as you are ready. It is very important that you do not feel you are being asked to give up your anorexia before you can begin the process of recovering. We all need our defences at different times in the course of our lives. We can only experiment with giving them up when we feel safe enough to do so.

People who work with anorexic women have the job of supporting and assisting in this task of rediscovering the self and learning to manage without the anorexia. They need to be able to understand and respect the solution which the anorexic woman has adopted, at the same time as caring for the woman within.

Finally, a word of warning. One difficulty which you may find in reading this book is how to make the connections between what I have to say in the first part, and what follows in the second.

In the first part I am concerned to place our understanding of anorexia in a very much wider social context than we usually do, embracing the vast complexities of all our relations to food and eating, the structures of power and industry which determine what kinds of foods we eat and produce as well as the effects of the shocking disparities between the eating habits of the affluent West and the hungry Third World. I lay some stress on the difficulties which girls and women have in finding a place in the worlds of work and education, and on the effect of prevailing notions of womanhood on our abilities to accept ourselves as both successful and feminine.

In the second part of the book, where I discuss how women who have become anorexic can help themselves and be helped to resume a more settled pattern of relations to their bodies and how they nourish them, I focus on much more personal matters, such as childhood, family relationships, the hopes, fears, ambitions and fantasies of the women concerned.

In other words, whereas the first part of the book might seem to imply the necessity of a *social* response to the problem of eating disorders, in the second part I offer an *individual* one.

This relationship between social and individual analyses is a very real problem. And slogans such as 'The personal is the political' do not take us far enough. Or, at least, not if we wish to change ourselves. We cannot expect the multinational companies who determine what we eat and how we look to change overnight. Nor for our confused and contradictory expectations of young women to miraculously straighten themselves out. This is no excuse for collectively leaving our world exactly as it is, but meanwhile, those women who are deeply troubled in their relations to their bodies must find a way to live in this world – not some other.

But even so, we should not be tempted to compartmentalise these two aspects of the problem, as if they were entirely separate. If we exclude the social world in our attempts to solve the difficulties of individuals, however deep we may delve into the psyche in the pursuit of causes and explanations, we shall never find them. Rather, I believe we must pluck our understandings from external *and* internal experience. The task then is to work with individuals at bringing those understandings alive in terms of their own experience.

2
A Strange Symptom in a Very Strange World

Almost everyone who has written about anorexia in recent years has recognised its connection with the current social obsession with slimming.[1] But if it is true that nowadays an enormous propaganda machine, combining the health services and private advertising, encourages people and women in particular to monitor closely their food intake, then it is even more true that in order to live, we all must eat.

As women, we have and have always had, a particularly profound and complex relationship to food, in terms of its production, supply and preparation as well as its consumption. In order to begin to understand how and why women develop eating disorders, we must first think about the vast complexities of the organisation of food production and food consumption in which women in general are caught up. Otherwise, we might easily fall into the trap of believing that it all begins and ends with slimming.

Food: big business and women's business

Food, in the Western world, has never before been available in such abundance and variety as it is today. We can hardly pass an hour of our lives without some reminder of its central importance. Eating is no longer a matter of subsistence. Every aspect of the activity supports a vast consumer industry manufacturing its specialist products. There are baby foods, children's foods, fast foods, convenience foods, whole foods and of course, slimming foods. Not only are we bombarded with products to buy, but also with articles, magazines and books about the products and about food philosophies.

Much of our social activity is conducted through the medium of food. Eating meals together, whether it is a spontaneous informal supper with friends or a formal dinner party, has always been an important part of the way we develop relationships. And though eating out – whether in a restaurant or the local pub – has never been more popular, still, as in grandmother's day, cooking and eating remain central to our conception of home life. Home is still judged by the amount and quality of the food produced and consumed there. Women still often judge ourselves and each other by the criterion of 'keeping a good table'.

Eating is indeed big business. Over three million people in the United Kingdom are employed in the catering industry alone. Add to them the numbers of people employed in the manufacture, processing and packaging of foods, and the economic dimensions look vast. But the food industry has a real problem built into it: as incomes rise, it has to try to persuade us to spend more of our money on its products, while there is a limit to the actual amount of food we are able to eat. We therefore have to be encouraged to buy more expensive foods and most importantly, foods which produce a higher level of profit for the manufacturer. The job of persuading us to buy processed, partially cooked potatoes instead of real ones, becomes a very serious undertaking. The amount of choice we actually have as consumers is limited by the concerns of advertising and marketing.[2]

All of this goes on for us in the West in the knowledge that a central problem of the world at present is its seeming inability to feed its own population. Food thus has a double edge for us. We may not be allowed to forget our own society's preoccuption with it, but we are continually reminded that our self-indulgence is at the expense of the other half of the globe. That is, of course, when we are not being told that we are all eating ourselves to death and that if we were to adopt a 'third world' diet, we should all live twice as long.

Small wonder that our relationship with the food we eat is a troubled one.

Women are the prime and generally exclusive targets of all the propaganda about food, both medical and commercial. Food in our society and in most others it seems, is regarded as the responsibility of women. It is one of the few areas of life in which we are expected to be in control. Responsibility for the provision of food does not just mean that we do the cooking (although within the home this is usually the case). Women spend very large amounts of time *thinking* about food, shopping, planning meals, studying the nutritional pros and cons of different foods and trying to reconcile these with other people's preferences, our own time and of course, the constraints of the family budget.

Ehrenreich and English[3] trace the history of the elevation of cooking and housewifery, once simply part of the background of life, to a scientific activity – a vocation for women! Domestic Science secured its hold on women by convincing us of the great responsibility we held and of all the perils and pitfalls involved in the creation and maintenance of a healthy family. As Anna Davin[4] has pointed out in her article on 'Imperialism and Motherhood', in late Victorian and Edwardian Britain, a huge amount of propaganda was also directed at women's even wider responsibilities to sustain a fit and healthy nation, and what was often called the 'manliness' of the 'Imperial Race'. If we pause for a moment to consider the amount of time and energy we still put into the planning of meals, in addition to the time spent actually buying and cooking the food, we could be forgiven for concluding that we have 'swallowed' all the propaganda, hook, line and sinker!

Food is the medium through which women demonstrate our love and concern for our children, lovers, husbands and friends. Even in families where men cook, they usually take on the role of chef. The woman still shops, plays the kitchen porter and washes up as well. Very few men, for example, cook the children's tea, or feel responsible if the family runs out of cornflakes or coffee. The feeding of babies and young children is considered such a fundamentally feminine activity that much of the literature on the subject uses the terms 'mother' and 'feeder' interchangeably.

In so far as food is necessary to life and health, women, by our control of the provision of it within the family, assume responsibility for the comfort, health and ultimately the lives of other people.

But eating is also a pleasurable activity. Feeding is one of the principal ways in which women please the people we care about. Taking care over the preparation of food is an act of love. In the same way, the refusal to eat someone's food can be a powerful statement of rejection. All children know this and food refusal is a traditional weapon in our culture in the small child's struggle for autonomy. It is because we understand its symbolic significance that many of us, even as grown women, have a great deal of difficulty in refusing any food our mothers offer – even if we do not really want to eat it.

To have a child who is a faddy eater is every mother's nightmare, although she may unwittingly encourage the behaviour by the lengths to which she will go to tempt her wayward offspring's appetite. She feels both worried and guilty if the child will not eat.

Guilt is an essential component in the role of women as feeders. And usually mothers cannot win. Somehow, modern Western society has contrived to put a spanner in the smooth workings of a woman's relationship with her children via food. Whatever we do, conflict seems to be built into our responsible role as feeders and carers. An example: Good nourishing food is what every mother knows her children need. She also knows it is usually the last thing they want. Give them junk food, and they will love you. But you will also have to live with the guilt about their teeth, their weight, their vitamins. Give them 'whole food', put up with their moanings, the waste, the unfavourable comparisons with other people's mothers, and you can take refuge in the fact that you really are a Good Mother – even though no one actually seems to have noticed!

This symbolic nurturing through feeding is a powerfully recurring theme in women's lives. Yet it is complicated, not so much by women ourselves, but by the conflicting pressures, posing as advice, guidance and education which surround it. As women, we are all subject to these alarming and contradictory authorities, the more so if we later become mothers. Those of us who do not go on to become anorexic inherit the same difficulties in our relationship with food as those of us who do. Those of us who do not have anorexic daughters still transmit our doubts and confusions to our offspring in the same way as those of us who do. We need to remember this when we read books on anorexia. Even Hilde Bruch,[5] who has made such a profoundly insightful and useful contribution to our understanding of the problem, tends to see the mothers of anorexic women as in some way different from 'ordinary' mothers. She sees the mothers of anorexic girls as generally over-concerned with their children's physical well-being, to the exclusion of other needs the children might have. She also suggests that they are rather over-anxious and over-solicitous about the nutritional needs of the children when they are very young. This may well be true; but in view of what has been said about women as feeders, we might expect it to be true for all 'good mothers' – not just those who have anorexic daughters! We read books about caring for our babies, the midwives and nurses tell us how to do it, the doctor tells us too, and so does the health visitor. Our own mothers, or other older women tell us yet again. What are we expected to be? Spontaneous?

So much for women as feeders. What of women as eaters? Here the situation is even more confused and riven with conflict.

As little girls, we learn to eat to please and reassure our mothers. Not to gratify or satisfy ourselves. When we ourselves become providers of food, it is once again to please and show concern for others. If women want to have a 'natural' and spontaneous relationship with food, if we want to eat for ourselves in our own right, we have to go to a lot of trouble to learn how to; it is not what we 'naturally' inherit.

At a recent workshop for women who consider themselves to have difficulties with food, I asked the question, 'How often do you buy and cook the food you would really like to eat?' The answer from all the women was, 'Almost never'. Even those women who did not have to cook for other people very rarely ate what they really would have liked. Eating was hedged around by a series of 'shoulds' and 'oughts', which had the effect of making it more a penance than a pleasure. Conversations with women who did not consider themselves to have particular difficulties with food revealed a similar picture. Many women said they avoided having their favourite foods in the house for fear of eating too much of them, though they always ensured that other people's preferences were well catered for.

So, it seems that eating is a source of pleasure, but not often for the people who have the primary responsibility for providing it. Women take control of food, while simultaneously denying ourselves the pleasure of it.

There was an intriguing television commercial shown some while ago which seems to embody the contradictions, at least in part. It consists of a woman dancing around a stage set, holding on high a steaming dish of a particular brand of frozen chips. She is singing that the man who is pursuing her loves her only for her chips. (They are not hers incidentally, but the food manufacturer's.) The man protests that he loves her for herself. She knows best however and lures him on with the smell of fried potatoes.

The really interesting thing about the advertisement is that the woman herself is extremely thin and obviously has not so much as looked at a chip in years.

So what is the message here for women? It is that we have a certain amount of power over men as providers of food. We can use this power in order to win love from them. The other part of our power is our ability to be sexually attractive and desirable. We can use this too to win men's love, but only if we do not ourselves eat the food we provide for them.

This advertisement works because it depicts symbolically what we already know. The message comes through to us from many directions. We saw our mothers feeding our fathers, but themselves watching what they ate. We see magazines full of tempting dishes for 'the family'! They are always followed by diets for us. And pictures of clothes designed for women of the 'ideal shape'.

What women are learning is that food is for everyone but us.

Food for the spirit : the ascetic tradition[6]

People who have not experienced anorexia usually believe that it begins with young women seeking to lose weight in order to make themselves more attractive in a purely 'cosmetic' sense. In fact, as those women who have been through an anorexic phase well know, it is rarely as simple as that. Some of you will not really remember how it all began, for others, the origins lie in a long-standing sense of dissatisfaction with life – which seems as though it may be solved by losing weight. Many of you will have initially lost weight by accident – perhaps as a result of an illness or a period of unhappiness.

By the time a woman reaches the point where her anorexic state is well established, she will not be especially interested in whether or not she is attractive to other people. Her own perceptions of herself and feelings about herself are really all that is important to her.

If young women who become anorexic are not starving themselves in pursuit of a cosmetic ideal, how are we to understand from within our own cultural experience what some of the factors involved might be?

There is within our culture a powerful but unrecognised element in the drive which so many people experience to control and limit their food intake. In other societies with a more overtly religious base, this element has been termed 'asceticism'. Fasting has always been a central practice within this tradition, either in the form of occasional and severe ritual fasts or the more prolonged limitation of food. In the Christian West, Lent is probably the last vestige of the prescribed fast. But what is this asceticism really about? Why do people do it?

We are all encouraged to regard self-denial as a 'good' thing. Self-indulgence is almost universally seen as a sign of moral weakness. In this respect self-indulgence in the area of food is put on a moral par with other forms of transgression. 'It's illegal, it's immoral or it makes you fat', and 'naughty but nice', are both familiar but powerful statements of this connection.

The ability to limit food intake and to lose weight bring with them a far-reaching moral kudos, with implications of will power and the capacity to 'resist temptation'.

In earlier cultures, self-denial in the area of food was always associated with the denial of sexual pleasure and gratification, both being regarded as 'sins of the flesh'. The so-called sexual revolution has now made sexual gratification almost obligatory. But the association between sexuality and food has not disappeared, it has merely been reshaped. In a quite straightforward way, a woman's sexual acceptability depends on her being slim.

The linking of sexual attractiveness with thinness in women is often regarded as a twentieth-century phenomenon; certainly women today are expected to conform to a narrower and more rigid stereotype than ever before. Yet in another more profound and less well-articulated sense, women's acceptability has always depended upon our ability to deny the body and to subdue it.

Asceticism, and the complex history of men's and women's attempts to achieve moral perfection rests on the notion of the dualism of body and spirit. The physical side of human nature is regarded as inherently sinful and impure. It always tends to drag down the aspiring spirit to the level of the impure or profane. The purpose of the practices of asceticism has been described as that of 'freeing the soul out of the prison of the body'.[7]

In the case of women, this dualism between body and spirit is in special ways fundamental to our socialisation. Women's bodies, much more so than men's, are regarded as impure, unclean and morally dangerous. The beliefs about the polluting effects of menstruation in so-called 'primitive' societies are well known.[8] However, it was not so many years ago that in our own culture a menstruating woman was barred from the dairy, lest she turn the cream sour.[9] In fact, ever since Eve tempted Adam to sin, women have lived under the shadow of our dangerous bodies. In the pursuit of moral worthiness, women must find a way to dissociate ourselves from our bodies.

Our bodies are, by their very nature, never totally controllable, and most of us will at some time have experienced our own bodies as malevolent, even alien to us. At puberty they begin to assume a shape of their own, independently of our will. Throughout our lives they continue to resist at least some of our attempts at control and regulation. The powerful social mythology which interprets women's 'uncontrollable' bodies not as something natural and miraculous, but rather as tempting and evil, simply serves to intensify and magnify our fear of ourselves.

Can we consider the possibility that becoming 'anorexic' involves us in taking the dualism between body and spirit literally? That the degree of guilt that a woman in an anorexic phase feels when she eats is not simply explained by her fear of becoming fat? That the desire and need to limit and control food intake represents a moral striving, an attempt to prove that she is morally and spiritually strong and worthwhile?

If such a woman sees herself and her body as two quite separate and distinct entities, she may believe that by abusing her body, she is doing 'herself' good. Her assaults upon her body cannot harm her. On the contrary, they can only make her better.

There is some evidence that anorexic women have a particularly strong sense of self-disgust with their own bodies. Hilde Bruch[10] mentions the difficulties her patients had in coming to terms with menstruation, and Sheila MacLeod[11] gives a memorable description of her own horror when her periods began. Anorexia has the effect not only of ridding the female body of its disturbing curves, it also causes a temporary halt in menstruation. This is probably as near to controlling her body as any woman is ever going to get! In addition, anorexia satisfies the moral need for self-denial. At least initially of course, weight loss also brings admiration from other people, for it appears to be conforming to the social injunction that women shall be thin. It is only when we begin to realise the subtle combination of women's needs which are met by anorexia that we can understand why it is such a seductive solution.

Unladylike – but distinctly feminine

There is yet one more strand in the social mythology which defines the relationship between women, our bodies and the food we eat. There is a real sense in which eating is itself regarded as an 'unfeminine' activity.

Aldous Huxley's novel, *Chrome Yellow*,[12] contains within it a little story which vividly depicts the ethereal quality, the other-worldliness which is such an important aspect of feminine charm. It is the story of the three Miss Lapiths. When George Wimbush goes for dinner with the Lapith family, he is struck by the spiritual beauty of the three daughters. What impresses him particularly is that throughout the meal they hardly eat anything. This is what they say when he comments on their apparent lack of appetite:

> 'Pray, don't talk to me of eating', said Emmeline, drooping like a sensitive plant. 'We find it so unspiritual, my sisters and I. One can't think of one's soul when one is eating!' . . .
> For his part, he thought them wonderful, wonderful, especially Georgiana. Georgiana was the most ethereal of all; of the three, she ate the least, swooned most often, talked most of death and was the palest. At any moment it seemed she might lose her precarious hold on this material world and become all spirit.

Mr Wimbush continues to adore his ethereal and unattainable Georgiana. One day, unable to control his passion, he goes uninvited to the Lapith residence. Creeping round, hoping to catch a glimpse of his beloved, he chances across a secret stairway. He follows it and it takes him to a room where he finds the three Miss Lapiths . . . eating, in a most abandoned manner! He blunders out in horror and Georgiana is so shamed that she agrees to marry him to ensure his silence.

Would Miss Georgiana Lapith have been unmarriageable if the story had got out that she was really mortal?

It seems that physical frailty, or at least a lack of physical vigour, is often held to be an attractive feminine quality. Ehrenreich and English give a startling account of the association between sickliness and femininity in the closing decades of the nineteenth century amongst the middle and upper classes in England and America. Sickness and invalidism became a way of life for so many women at that time that it would not be an exaggeration to describe the phenomenon as an epidemic. They note that, 'A morbid aesthetic developed, in which sickness was seen as a source of female beauty, and beauty – in the high fashion sense – was in fact a source of sickness. Over and over, nineteenth-century romantic paintings feature the beautiful invalid, sensuously drooping on her cushions, eyes fixed tremulously at her husband or physician, or already gazing into the Beyond.'[13]

It is difficult to resist the parallel between the cult of invalidism described in the nineteenth century and the epidemic of anorexia which afflicts privileged young women in our own. The nineteenth-century malaise was given a variety of labels.[14] The symptoms of the disorder were certainly not identical with those we observe in anorexia, although the effects of the two are remarkably uniform. Both render useless women who might otherwise be in a position to lead useful and challenging lives. Both are disorders of affluence rather than of want. Both involve an ambivalent kind of conformity to a romantic ideal of the frail and spiritual being who is in imminent danger of wasting away. Both incidentally provide the chance of fame and fortune for a good many male 'experts' who offer treatment, but rarely cures, for the unfortunate women.

Earlier on, I suggested that eating itself was in the past considered to be an 'unfeminine' activity. 'But surely', some women may argue, 'we have outgrown all that. It may have been true once, but after two decades of Women's Liberation, surely women are at least allowed to eat?'

No, I am afraid we are not! In a recent group of bulimic women with which I was involved, it was unanimously asserted by the women that they thought of eating as essentially unfeminine. They weren't talking about over-eating, but eating itself. Many women who would not describe themselves as having particular problems with food share the same feelings about eating and femininity. 'I have quite a good appetite really, but if I'm out with a new boyfriend, I always pick at my food – you know, as if I wasn't really interested in food. I mean, it's not very romantic really to eat like a pig, is it?'

Perhaps Kim Chernin is right in her powerful account of the tyranny of slenderness, *Womansize*. She believes that not only has the women's movement failed to help to make our images of womanhood more realistic, but on the contrary, it has contributed to the very opposite. She says, 'I am suggesting that the changing awareness among women of our position in this society has divided itself into two divergent movements, one of which is a movement towards feminine power, the other a retreat from it, supported by the fashion and diet industries which share a fear of women's power.'[15]

Dressed to kill: the consequence of fashion?

The time has come to have a more rigorous look at the world of women's fashion, which is so often accused of being at the root of all our ills.

It is probably true to say that for as long as records of fashion have been kept, women have been expected and required to conform to the prevailing physical stereotypes. This is nothing new. From the Chinese practice of binding the feet of girl children to keep them small, to the wasp-waists of our Elizabethan ancestors, fashion has rarely meant anything as simple as just wearing the right clothes. It usually also entails the changing of women's bodies to look good in them. Fashion never stands still; one season's clothes may demand full breasts and tiny waists, while the next year, the flat-chested look might be the order of the day. No one ever doubts that somehow, as if by magic, we women will succeed in changing ourselves to comply.

Can we then hope that the present preference for straight lines, flat chests and the complete absence of stomachs and bottoms is simply a fashion fad which will pass? Can we hope for a return to a stereotype of womanhood which will allow us to abandon our cheese salads and eat potatoes again?

Perhaps it will not be as simple as all that. Thinness is more than a mere fashion stereotype. It is of course, much appreciated by the fashion industry, because if one wants to emphasise the clothes rather than the woman, it is a great help if she closely resembles a coat hanger. Fashion models are thin so that we will notice their clothes unhindered by the contours of their bodies. But the requirement that women conform to a remarkably lean stereotype is not a responsibility to be laid solely at the feet of the clothes manufacturers. Simply to say that it is fashionable to be thin does not explain the peculiar endurance of this physical pattern, neither does it account for the profound importance which thinness has for us all.

If we look at the way women are portrayed in the media, it is clear that not only is thinness presented as attractive, but when women are represented as in some sense successful, they are always shown to be thin. From the mother in the kitchen speaking ecstatic words of praise for a particular brand of detergent to the carefree young woman executive, women who are shown as successful are also shown to be thin.

From early in our childhoods, we tend to associate social and career success with thinness. Research has indicated the marked preference shown by very young children for images representing thin as opposed to plump children.[16] Not only do the children express a preference for the appearance of thin bodies, but they also prefer to be physically close to thin people. The thin images, the children associated with being popular, smart and good at sport, while the plumper shapes are thought to be stupid and, more importantly, lonely. Small wonder that the relentless pursuit of thinness we call anorexia should afflict children at earlier and earlier ages.

These attitudes continue throughout childhood and into adolescence. Early on in life the prejudices against fat people are shared equally by boys and girls and are directed against both sexes. Quite soon however it becomes clear that they are focused on girls' bodies. As we learn our hatred of fat people so early on in life it is not surprising that by the time they reach adolescence, many young people have a morbid fear of becoming fat. By this stage girls demonstrate much more anxiety than boys about the size and shape of their bodies. This level of anxiety is not surprising when we consider the conclusions of a study by Monello and Mayer.[17] They suggest that the prejudice against fat people is similar to that directed against certain racial minorities. They also conclude that fat people themselves suffer the same damage to their self-esteem and share the same resistance to achievement as that found amongst racial minorities who are subject to social hatred and discrimination. The effect of these negative images and associations with fat is to make us overvalue thinness.

Susie Orbach is absolutely correct when she says, 'We know that every woman wants to be thin. Our images of womanhood are synonymous with thinness. If we are thin, we shall feel healthier, lighter and less restricted. Our sex lives will be easier and more satisfying . . . When we are fat, we crave the thinness as we crave the food, searching within it for the solution to our varied problems.'[18]

But I am not content to leave it here. Yes, we loathe and stigmatise fat people, the very idea of fat arouses our negative feelings. In consequence, we are all afraid of becoming fat. As young women in particular, unsure enough anyway about our own capacity to be acceptable, to 'fit' in the world, we are apt to consider that to become fat is probably the worst thing on earth which could happen to us. But why? Why is it *fat* that we all get into such a state about?

I can only understand this curious phenomenon by assuming that fat, and fat people, are used by our society as the emotional dumping ground for all kinds of aspects of ourselves and of our culture which we do not want to own. To put it another way, we collectively project on to fatness bad qualities which really do not belong to it at all, but to ourselves. Then all we have to do is to avoid being fat, and we are safe from the very worst of ourselves.

Some examples. We project our greed on to fat people. We believe that fat people must necessarily eat more than thin people, and we insist on maintaining this belief, despite evidence to the contrary.

Garrow in 1974[19] reviewed the findings of thirteen studies which looked at the relationship between weight and food intake. Twelve out of the thirteen studies revealed that the overweight subjects ate either the same amount or less than thin subjects. And yet no one really believes a fat person who says that she does not over-eat. We need to know that fat people are greedy. Our culture regards greediness as a highly undesirable quality, and yet we must be the greediest civilisation ever to have existed. We define our needs in such a way that people in other parts of the world must actually starve in order that they shall be met. This is not an individual kind of greediness. It will not help the proverbial starving millions if I, individually, go without my dinner. But we are all involved in a collective greediness so serious that it amounts to genocide. Thank heaven for fat people. All the time they are around, we can be quite sure that it is not our fault.

Sometimes, we even insist in believing the double nonsense that fat people are both greedy and lazy. And yet obesity is much more common amongst the poorer social classes than it is amongst the rich. Perhaps human beings need to be really confident that there is enough to go round before we can indulge in the luxury of self-denial! Poorer people also seem to have a greater tolerance of fatness. In a study by Goodman et al,[20] the only group of children who did not rank the overweight child last in order of desirability were a sample from a poor Jewish community. The authors speculate that, 'the well-fed, stockily-built Jewish child is often viewed by other Jews as one who is both healthy and *loved*.'

For the past few years, the medical profession has rallied to reinforce the prevailing social prejudices in respect of fat people. While acknowledging that to be very much heavier than most other people might well be a health hazard, I find it disturbing that women who are only a few pounds 'overweight' are often shamed by their doctors into going on diets. Even literature which we might expect to take a fairly enlightened view of the matter fails to examine the assumption that 'overweight' is to blame for all manner of human ills.

Isobel Contento in her article on 'The Nutritional Needs of Women'[21] says, 'Since we often do not decrease food intake or increase exercise, it is no wonder that some one-third of all Americans today are obese. And so many diseases are prevalent among obese individuals – heart disease, diabetes, and hypertension, to name just a few – that the maintenance of normal weight is probably the greatest single contributor to good health.'

On the other hand research exists which indicates that there is little if any relationship between ill-health and overweight as such. The perpetual roundabout of eating followed by starvation, which is the pattern so many women feel pressured to follow, may be more damaging to health than overweight.[22]

It is at present impossible to decide upon 'the real truth' about the relationship between health and weight. And yet we are so convinced that in addition to all their moral failings, fat people are also killing themselves, that we never stop to consider the evidence.

Adelle Davis, the great American nutritionist, who died in 1974, has some strong words to say on the matter.

> Physicians are realising that reducing is not for everyone . . . regardless of how much they hate being overweight, they are healthier because of it. When these persons force themselves to reduce, they often have emotional breakdowns, suffer from marked depression . . . are overcome with guilt, disgust and self-hatred at being weak and gluttonous. If possible, such people should forget about reducing and strive to build health. They are usually cheerful, witty, intelligent individuals who make a worthwhile contribution to society . . . The attitude that a slender person is somehow more acceptable than an overweight one is ridiculously immature. Unless you happen to have a husband who for ego-building purposes wishes to display you as he would a new Cadillac, there is little reason for looking like a mannequin. Overweight persons can dress attractively; and many individuals with a 'lean and hungry look' are not pretty in bathing suits either.[23]

Why women?

Before we leave the complex subject of fat and thin and of our attitudes to it, we must ask the final question: Why is it women who have taken on the social problem of fatness and thinness? Why is it women, much more than men, who are frightened of becoming fat? Why do women so readily accept the nonsense which we project on to them about the size and shape of their bodies?

The answers are simple, but also complex; they are related both to the availability of women's bodies to the public gaze and to the sense of powerlessness and the need for approval which women experience in our own society.

Women are, in a real sense, the sex which we all look at. There is a social expectation which small girls learn at a very early age, that we as women will strive to make ourselves attractive to other people.

When we go to parties or attend other social occasions, we are well aware that our clothes, our hair, our figures may be looked at and commented upon. Even in the course of our work, people will often form an initial impression of us through our appearance; our actual achievements may be of secondary importance. Even women who achieve high office and become national figures by virtue of their achievements, still find that the press will concentrate as much on their outfits as upon their speeches. A woman who is fat is therefore very likely to be noticed and criticised for it. Indeed, any woman whose body falls short of the narrow prescription which our culture imposes, is likely to feel vulnerable and at a distinct disadvantage.

As girls we are socialised from the earliest age to rely to a great extent on the approval of other people. We are taught to please, and to feel good when people approve of us. Our sense of *self*-esteem is based less upon our own assessment of ourselves and our achievements than upon the opinions of others, and how readily we please them. The woman who is 'overweight' is very unlikely therefore to be able to maintain a positive image of herself. She tends to measure her own worth in terms of other people's responses to her and their responses will be directed more towards her appearance than anything else. We are therefore quite literally tyrannised by the fear of fatness and it is small wonder that the vast industry involved in the production of so-called slimming aids finds a ready market amongst women. In our culture, an individual needs a very firm sense of self and a very high self-esteem to be able to resist the social pressures to be thin.

3
Identifying Anorexic Women

If you are at present in the middle of an anorexic episode, or if you have had the experience in the past, you may well wonder what it is about you which led you towards this particular set of difficulties. Families with an anorexic member often ask the same question: 'Why did this happen to our daughter? Why our family?'

In this chapter, we can only begin to look at these questions in a general way. We can try to discover what kind of woman *most often* develops anorexia. Generalisation can be dangerous – there are always exceptions to general patterns – but they are also useful.

The importance of looking at the kinds of people who fall prey to a particular disorder or difficulty is twofold.

First, it may make the problem predictable and therefore preventable. Second, it may tell us something about the nature and origins of the problem itself.

But before we go further, a warning: a study of the people who become anorexic can indicate to us which groups of people in our society are particularly vulnerable, but it is unlikely to be able to tell us which people will in fact become anorexic – just as, if we study those people who present themselves for treatment for depression, we can learn which groups of people are most vulnerable to it, without being able to specify which vulnerable individuals will actually become depressed.

Similarly with anorexia. The information we can glean about the sorts of people who develop anorexia will probably only alert us to the risks which certain groups run. It will not point to specific individuals. In terms of understanding more about the nature and origins of anorexia however, a study of the 'anorexic population' can provide us with a great deal of help. Social medicine has traditionally begun with a study of the lives of those people it seeks to treat. Diseases caused by polluted water were well on the way to being cured when researchers observed that a number of people using the same water supply contracted the disease at the same time. When it comes to research into problems which affect the human mind or spirit, drawing such deductions is more difficult. However, it can be done. The observations of Brown and Harris in their study of depression in women reveal that very many London women are depressed, whereas in the Hebrides, depression is unknown.[1] This should tell us something, or at least stimulate some further questioning. It should tell us that depression in women is related more to the social worlds in which they exist than it is to their own neurotic tendencies. The task then becomes one of looking at the different variables involved in life in one place and life in another and trying to establish what exactly produces the problem in one place and fails to produce it in another. This is what we shall do with anorexia. We will try to use the information we have about women who are defined as anorexic to ask some fruitful questions about anorexia.

Geographical distribution: a problem only in the West?

Anorexia is reported as prevalent throughout the 'developed' world. It occurs in apparently increasing numbers in Europe, North America, Australasia, South Africa, Japan and some of the Gulf States. It occurs, in fact, wherever there is enough to eat and where in addition, thinness is prized. We must of course approach these observations and many other statistical 'facts' about anorexia with caution. In societies without a well-developed medical service and with a certain expectation of starvation for economic reasons, anorexia would be unlikely to be recognised even if it existed. But even with that warning in mind, the fact that anorexia is not reported *at all* in the third world should allow us to assume that it is indeed a problem associated with affluence. In addition, we looked in Chapter 2 at the ways in which contemporary western societies try to deal with the difficulties they experience in relation to their own affluence. It certainly appears that eating disorders, especially amongst women, would be much more likely to appear in relatively affluent situations.

A problem only for young women?

In the popular imagination, anorexia nervosa is inevitably associated with young women. In this instance, the popular image is, on the whole, correct. Let us take the question of sex and gender first. Anorexia, like other eating disorders, is overwhelmingly a woman's problem. The reported proportions of women to men vary from one writer to another, but most report a ratio higher than 10:1.[2]

We are accustomed to the idea that some illnesses are more prevalent in one sex than the other. Heart disease for example, claims far more men for its victims than it does women. Psychological disorders (or at least, those which doctors see and treat) are much more common amongst women. In the case of anorexia, it is hard to think of another problem which selects one sex so overwhelmingly. It might be tempting to wonder whether perhaps it is *necessary* to be female to develop anorexia. Whether perhaps either physically or psychologically only women are able to develop it. This assumption was made by some of the psychoanalytical writers on the subject in the 1940s.[3] The explanation they gave was that anorexia nervosa resulted from a fear of oral impregnation. (Being made pregnant through the mouth.) This is clearly an explanation which can only apply to women. We are now in a position to conclude that any theory couched in terms of the unique biology or psychology of women must be wrong. The fact is that although we do not see many anorexic men, we do see *some*. And the ones we do see conform just as fully to the pattern we have come to associate with anorexia as do the women. So anorexia is not a disorder exclusive to women; men can get it too. But it is a problem to which women are very much more vulnerable than men.

Similarly, when we look at the age profile of anorexic women, we will see that the majority of them are indeed young – but by no means all. According to Dally[4] the commonest age at which weight loss began in his sample was 15. It is often said that 18 is the average age of onset of anorexia.[5] It is certainly not unknown for women to develop the problem in their late 20s, early 30s or even later. We have treated a number of women who developed the problem after some years of marriage and after the birth of children. These women however are in the minority. It is far more common for women to develop anorexia in their teens or early twenties.

In order to illustrate what these women from a considerable age range have in common, it will be easiest to describe some of their lives and draw our conclusions from there.

Nicola was diagnosed as having anorexia when she was 17 years old and was seen by the counselling service while still an A-level student at a local girls boarding school. The story she told is unusual, but in some respects very typical of young women who develop an anorexic disorder. Nicola came from a professional family of four children. She initially described her family as 'very close, very supportive – no problems at all'. It transpired that her parents had in fact divorced when she was 11. She was the next to youngest child and the youngest girl. She lived with her brothers and sister with her father and stepmother. Nicola's childhood had been considered a great success. She appeared to cope fairly well with the domestic disruption, formed a good relationship with her stepmother and, in addition, was 'brilliant' at school. Her intelligence was highly valued by her parents, who had great hopes for her and very much wanted her to win the Oxford scholarship which her teachers assured them she was capable of doing. It was after she had gained an impressive array of O-levels that she began to lose weight and developed a stubborn refusal to eat food that might remotely be considered to be fattening.

In therapy, she began to reveal that the break-up of her parents' marriage had indeed caused her a great deal of distress. Nicola however felt a strong sense of loyalty to the reconstructed family and firmly believed that it was up to her to make it work. 'I feel so awful about worrying them like this. I know my father thinks it's his fault, because of the divorce and everything. But it really isn't. My stepmother has been really wonderful about it all, but I know she doesn't understand what it's all about and thinks there must be something wrong with the family.'

Nicola felt that her own bad feelings about the break-up of her parents' marriage would only upset her father and stepmother. She had never been one to make selfish demands on people and so she had resolved to make the best of it. Her compliant manner and also her academic success made her her father's favourite and life on the whole did not seem too bad. At 14 she had been sent to boarding school so that she could have every opportunity to fulfil her academic aspirations. It was at this point that she realised she was quite unable to cope with life away from her family. She continued to do well at her school work and to behave well, but she was quite unsure why she did so. She realised that she had no autonomous motivation for working. She continued to do it because it was expected of her, but found that the other students did not reward her efforts in the way her family had done. She successfully completed her O-levels, lost some weight in the process and felt suddenly that the real identity and sense of personal self-worth which had eluded her was at last at hand. 'To be absolutely honest, losing weight is really the only thing which is important. I don't know why, but I'd give up everything before that.'

Nicola was able eventually to understand that, prior to her anorexic episode, she had succeeded in dealing with life, but at the expense of developing any positive sense of who she was. She had seen herself simply as a being for other people, whose personality and destiny was shaped by their needs of her, rather than by anything she was or wanted for herself.

Marjorie came for help with her eating disorder when she was 23. She said that she had left home at 18 to go to college in London. She had successfully completed her teacher training and stayed an extra year to do her degree. She had become acutely anorexic during her first year in a teaching job, although she later came to see that she had had difficulties with food during her final year at college. When she first came for therapy, she was angry and confused by her own behaviour. 'I'm such an idiot. I had so much luck, everything was going right and now I'm throwing it all away.' She said she had not liked teaching (in fact, she said she was no good at it) in contrast to college which she had 'adored'.

It turned out that college itself had not been easy. Marjorie found it difficult to structure her life and time, and had dealt with this by developing a variety of routines, rituals even, which included a great deal of hard work. She did not believe that her considerable academic achievements were 'real'. They gave her no satisfaction. She had done well because she worked harder than other students. She was popular, but she had worked at this too. In short, Marjorie had built her achievements on a most fragile and unsatisfactory sense of self-esteem. When she left college, she had a real crisis about her own autonomy and felt completely unable to lead an independent and 'grown-up' life. Her eating began to go out of control. The rituals and routines which had protected her so well at college began to turn in on her. She would buy large quantities of food – usually the kind of food she did not like – and shut herself away to eat it all. This would be followed by making herself sick and sometimes by repeating the whole process over again. In a curious way, Marjorie's bulimic rituals gave her days a kind of focus which they seemed to lack without them.

Suzanne was 31 when she came for therapy. She presented herself as a dull and depressed housewife, who distinguished herself only by the fact that she was exceptionally thin. She had married at age 19 and now had a son of 11 and a daughter of 8. It transpired that she had come from a rather poor home, had won a place at the local grammar school and then at a college. She had given this up in order to get married. Her early years of marriage and motherhood were happy and successful. It was when both children were at school and Suzanne began a clerical job that she started to reflect upon her life and became preoccupied with her weight. She felt totally passive about her life, that it was quite out of her own control and that she could not make even the smallest decision on her own behalf. 'There's nothing wrong with my life at all. It's *me*. I don't really seem to be a person. I need other people for everything.'

Suzanne's mother she described as a loving but domineering woman. Her husband, although cheerful and obviously concerned for her, was also a powerful and controlling person. He was certainly not her intellectual equal. Suzanne's life up to the point of her anorexic episode had been based on pleasing other people: first her mother, then later her husband and children. She had never found the space to develop her own sense of competence or independence to deal with the world as an adult. It was not until she reached the age of 31 that she was actually able to find the psychological space to notice!

A question of identity

What Marjorie, Suzanne and Nicola have in common is clearly not age, nor is there any particular similarity in life circumstances between the three of them. They are linked though in that all three had reached a point in their own lives where issues about autonomy, independence and self-esteem had come to a head. Nicola had to face the fact that she must either continue with her rather brilliant academic career for her own sake or not at all. Marjorie had managed to make a success of college, but now found herself unable to use the success she had striven for in the sense of becoming an independent working woman. In Suzanne's case, she no longer had the demands of a young family to cope with and had to confront herself for the first time as an adult woman in her own right. She felt as though there was nothing there.

These are three examples. In all the anorexic women I have worked with, I have found a similar pattern. When together we reconstruct the situation they encountered at the time when the difficulties began, we find that they were caught up in a struggle for autonomy with which they felt unable to cope. This, of course, helps to explain why so many women develop an anorexic eating disorder at or around adolescence. Adolescence is a time in life when young people are encountering the possibilities of their own independence for the first time. It is also a time when young people begin to question their own identity. We often hear people referring to 'identity crises'. But what does such a term really mean? 'Identity' is best understood as a sense of self which involves both an acknowledgement and acceptance of individuality, of the uniqueness of ourselves, together with the feeling of being part of and accepted by a wider group. An identity crisis occurs when we feel in a great deal of conflict about who we are both as individual separate people and about where we stand in relation to other people. We all experience this kind of crisis at various points during our lives. It is only when the conflict seems quite impossible for us to resolve that we are likely to deal with it by developing a symptom such as anorexia.

Looking back to our three examples, it is clear that for different reasons, all three women had had earlier experiences which made it difficult for them to have a clear sense of who they were and of their own competence to manage life on their own terms.

Nicola had used her academic aptitude to win the approval of her family and had felt obliged to put their needs before her own. In consequence, she had not developed a strong sense of self and a belief in her own autonomy as a person which might otherwise have carried her through the separation from her family. It is worth noting that in the cases of very many women who go through an anorexic phase, their lives up until that time have appeared to other people to be remarkably problem-free. Mothers often describe daughters who 'were never any trouble until all this happened', 'the only one in the family who never gave me any worry' etc. This kind of behaviour preceding the disorder is not always the case, but it is common. The group of anorexics who 'never had any problems' fail to develop a strong sense of themselves as separate individuals because they always accept other people's definitions of themselves and never form their own. Many of the difficulties which children and adolescents cause in families are a reflection of the process of becoming independent. There is a real sense in which we need to fight against our parents' values and ideas if we are going to be able to develop our own. The young person who continues to accept her parents' view of the world and her parents' and teachers' definition and expectations of herself is failing to go through this process.

In Marjorie's case, she managed to go through the motions of becoming independent; she left home, succeeded at college but not far beneath the surface was the terrible gulf of doubt that she was really able to live her own life at all. She 'coped' by throwing herself into work; she defended herself against the fears of rejection by her peers by working hard at being popular, by studying what other people said and thought and wore and by imitating them accurately. When she came into therapy, she felt that her whole life had been a sham – and in a sense, she was right.

Suzanne had been a good girl – a quality which her mother prized most highly. There had never been any conflict between the two of them. She married young and spent many more years winning the approval of others by caring for them and by putting their needs before her own. Indeed, for a long time she could not even acknowledge that she had any needs apart from meeting theirs. For Suzanne, being loved and accepted meant doing what other people expected of her. She felt a great deal of guilt if she even wanted to do something for herself. All the time she was meeting other people's needs she was secure and felt loved. She had never had the experience of being loved and valued for *herself*, for what she actually was as a separate person in her own right and so she was terrified of being that person.

If we now look back to the fact that the vast majority of people who develop anorexic disorders are women, we can begin to see some of the reasons why. Little girls, more than little boys, are brought up to be 'good'. Passivity and compliance are qualities which are valued highly in girls whereas in boys a certain amount of resistance and rebellion is regarded as healthy. Compliant, passive and unselfish daughters may make for a tranquil family life; such a training however does not lead to a smooth passage to independence!

It is probably fair to assume that everyone at some time in their lives, both women and men, encounter difficulties with independence and feel that demands are being made upon them which they are unable to meet. It is much more likely however that boys will have had a training early on in life which will have equipped them to deal effectively with such demands. They are less likely to have a self-esteem which is based upon pleasing other people.

We might say then that anorexia often occurs as a response to a crisis about autonomy and independence. Women are less likely than men to be able to resolve such conflicts and are therefore more likely to be driven to producing symptoms such as anorexia. This kind of crisis can occur at any stage in life when issues related to independence are experienced particularly acutely. Adolescence is a common time for young women to experience these difficulties but it is by no means the only possible time.

Social class and education: a problem only for the middle class?

It has often been said that anorexia affects many middle-class young women. Palmer[5] says that 'on the whole it does seem more likely that anorexia is more common in the middle and upper classes'. He acknowledges that this may be the result of referral patterns and that anorexia occurring in 'working class' girls may sometimes be overlooked.

Dally and Gomez[6] mention that 77 percent of their sample are from social classes 1 and 2. They suggest that family pressure to succeed may be an important factor in anorexia and this pressure may occur more often in social classes 1 and 2.

My own observations are based on work with some 75 women suffering from anorexia, seen at a voluntary counselling agency and in the Health Service. Our work suggests that there may be a confusion in the literature between social class and educational achievement. We found that although many of the women who came to us for help were from middle-class backgrounds, others had parents who were manual workers who could not be considered in any sense to be middle class. What we did find however was that almost all the anorexic women had themselves done well educationally – whether or not they came from a middle-class background. Only two of the women seen by us had not achieved at least O-levels in the education system and most had A-levels as well. The confusion is an obvious one; in our society, middle-class people are much more likely to do well at school than working-class children are and so there is a tendency to confuse educational success with middle-class status. In our own sample, we were surprised by the rather large number of women who came from working-class back-grounds in which they were the first people to do well at school. Nineteen of the women in our sample were the first members of their family to go to college. This might lead us to suspect that women who come from backgrounds which do not particularly encourage educational achievement are more likely than other women to develop an anorexic disorder if they themselves are successful in education. We can be quite sure however that the women who do develop an anorexic condition are in general unusually talented intellectually and have often been marked out at an early age as high achievers. It is sad that the anorexic phase itself often intervenes to put an end to the woman's educational success. It is often while she is in the process of studying for O-levels, A-levels or her degree that the women enters this phase and often has to postpone or even abandon her career.

In order to understand why educated women are more likely to develop an anorexic disorder than are women who do not succeed in education, we must turn again to the idea of 'identity'. We need to look not at the parental pressure to succeed or the stress of the examination system, which are often blamed for anorexia, but at the identity confusion and conflict caused by the educational success itself. In our society, we pay lip service to the idea of equal opportunities for men and women. We say that girls have as much right to an education as boys have and we claim to give them the opportunity to exercise that right. What we fail to do however is to prepare young women for the experience of work success and independence. Little girls are brought up in different ways from little boys. Recent research indicates that apart from sex-typing children in terms of their clothes and toys, parents do not seem overtly to treat their girl and boy children very differently. But they do believe that girl and boy children *are* different, and they do have different expectations of them.[7] Even in the case of small babies, parents describe their daughters as gentle, loving, pretty and cuddly, whereas boy babies tend to be described as tough, rough, alert, active and intelligent. This means that different tendencies are encouraged in boys and girls. The outgoing, independent aspect of a small boy's personality will actually be elicited by his parents, while they similarly seek and find those aspects of the little girl which have to do with gentleness, caring and nurturing. Girls are encouraged to find satisfaction through affiliation; they learn to find their rewards in relationship with other people. The kinds of toys which girls are given to play with encourage them to use their nurturing capacities. In short, they are socialised into the idea of being a carer – a wife and mother. These are very subtle processes which take place very early on in a child's life. By the time she goes to school, the little girl will already be identifying herself as a woman-to-be and will understand her role very much in terms of caring and responding rather than acting and initiating. Girls who fail to learn these lessons are regarded as abnormal.

Once they get to school, little girls *are* encouraged to work hard and to do well. But they have already learnt that their 'proper' role in the world is that of future wife and mother. All of the girl's responses to education and career opportunity are tempered by that very early learning – reinforced of course by social expectation and by the stereotypes which surround her.

Girls do well at primary school – better, on the whole, than boys. They work harder, are more careful and conscientious than boys.

(Although as Dale Spender[8] points out, teachers tend to rate work more highly if they believe a boy has done it.)

The little girl's greater commitment to school work and to 'doing well' is easily explained in terms of what she has learnt to be acceptable behaviour. Girls have learnt to please, to comply and to give people what they expect. They simply transfer the same rules to school that they have learnt at home. Boys, on the other hand, have learnt that it is all right to be a bit wayward and adventurous, to sometimes disobey, to 'mess about' rather than work.

It is when they reach secondary school that the achievement of many girls begins to fall off and they tend to do less well than boys. It is a common phenomenon that girls of around 13 and 14 begin to take work less seriously. They become 'silly', 'giggly', more interested in clothes and make-up than in homework. The girls who do this are responding to the strong social expectations of what girls 'should' be like. They are reassuringly asserting that they are not going to be strong and independent, a challenge or a threat to men. Instead, they are becoming 'feminine'; essentially attractive and charming but unserious people.

But our concern is with those girls who do not become silly and unserious when they reach adolescence. They are the group in which most potential anorexics are to be found. For the girls who fall into this group, the forming of a positive adult identity will almost always be problematic. All girls are socialised into a sexual identity centred on motherhood, regardless of whether or not they later also have the opportunity to achieve educational success and make their own careers. To take education seriously not only conflicts with the injunction that motherhood is the primary component of female sexuality, it actually threatens the girl with a sexual identity which is negative and in general disapproved of. The common stereotypical images of the successful woman are not very encouraging. We have on the one hand the image of the business woman. The Director of IBM. A former Prime Minister even. Hard, ruthless, selfish. Superficially glamorous, maybe, but essentially unfit for marriage and motherhood. On the other hand, we have the image of the Bluestocking. The asexual woman, the spinister. Isolated, plain and lonely, who has spent 'the best years of her life' in some dry and ultimately unrewarding pursuit.

Neither of these stereotypes presents the clever adolescent girl with a very hopeful image with which to identify.

But, we might question, do not some adolescent girls at least have a more promising role model in the form of their mothers?

The fact is that many do not feel they have. Many daughters see their mothers as women who have done 'the right thing' and have abandoned their own chances of career success and fulfilment in order to care for a family. Even those daughters whose mothers have made what others may see as a successful compromise between their professional and personal lives may see them in a light very different from the outside world, or even the mother herself. Miranda, a 14-year-old girl, just released from hospital following an anorexic crisis, was talking to me about her own future and her confusions about it. 'The main thing is, I couldn't bear to be like my mother.' (Mother was a single parent and successful career woman who sounded to me quite admirable.) 'She works so hard. She has *so* much responsibility. I couldn't stand that. She's always tired and she's so guilty about *everything*.'

Perhaps we know our mothers better than they think.

If we do not have a positive picture of ourselves as people in the future, it is difficult for us to know who to be in the present. As girls, if we are doing well at school and are told that we have a good future ahead of us, we can often only see a bewildering array of contradictions.

Anorexia can be viewed as a way of stepping outside of this painful situation. When a woman feels unhappy and confused with her life, she will often tend to blame this on her physical imperfections; losing weight is a familiar way of dealing with depression. But a woman in an anorexic phase is aiming for much more than this. She is seeking the kind of physical perfection which will give her a positive sense of herself, at least in the present.

Anorexia is a paradoxical expression of the dilemmas which educated women face. On the one hand, the ability to lose weight and to exercise such rigorous self-control is a sign of strength and inner power. On the other hand, the anorexic woman by her childlike frailty is expressing the fact that she is not ready and able to take on the confusing responsibilities of independence.

4

Anorexic Women and Their Families

Much has been written in recent years about the role of the family in anorexic disorders. Some writers have suggested that the 'causes' of anorexia lie within the family; others have looked at the ways in which certain patterns of family behaviour can perpetuate the problem and make it more difficult for the anorexic member to give up her symptoms. Many of the families I have worked with have read about anorexia and have come across these ideas so that they have come for help already feeling as though they were responsible for the problem.

My own belief however is that any approach which seeks to blame families, or which makes families feel blamed, is both unthinking and unjust. It is unthinking because it offers no analysis of the 'family' itself. What do we mean by a 'family'? Only a minority of families in Britain in the 1980s and 1990s comprise the traditional mother/father/ children living together. Some of the rest may be 'reconstituted nuclear' after divorce, but many more are single-parent, or single-sex families. I am using the term 'family' to mean the group of whatever adults and children share the anorexic woman's home. But before going any further I want to make it clear that I am aware that a 'family' may represent a whole set of variable power relationships; and that in the classical nuclear family in our culture, the father represents 'authority' and the mother 'nurturing'. This pattern has consequences for both mothers and daughters, some of which are analysed later in this chapter. But in terms of the argument that blames families for the anorexic condition of daughters, we are really referring to the family in its nurturing role – that is, to *mothers*. It is essentially a mother-blaming attitude, which is doubly unjust, since mothers too are subject to the contradictions in our society's attitudes to women that we have already described.

So in reading this chapter, it is well to keep in mind that behind the word 'family' lurks the word 'mother'.

Mothers have often commented to me that the attitudes of medical and nursing staff have encouraged them to feel that they are responsible for their daughters' difficulties. But they also feel that if they ask questions, this is construed as meddling, interfering with the treatment. One mother, when she expressed concern over her daughter's distress at being subjected to a rigid refeeding programme, was actually told by a ward sister that this kind of overprotective 'fussing' was what had led to her daughter's breakdown in the first place. It is easy, standing at a distance, to see that such a comment is made not only through insensitivity but through sheer ignorance. It is much more difficult to apply that sort of perspective to a comment when it is directed at you!

To say that blaming families is probably the least helpful stance that a therapist can take, is not to say that families are uninvolved in the problem. Most of our important experience as human beings is mediated through our families. The family is our direct route to the social world. I think it is true to say that we can never understand another person without reference to their family and that no one truly understands herself until she understands something of her relationship to her family.

In this chapter, we shall review the research and speculation which exists on the kinds of families which anorexics come from. I will hope to offer further thoughts on the matter and will focus in particular on the relationships between mothers and daughters.

But to begin, we must consider the sorts of difficulties which anorexic women create for their families.

All parents know, to some extent, how difficult it is to live with a child who will not eat. At some stage in their development, often before they go to school, most children seem to go through a phase in which they are extremely difficult to feed. It may be that they will only eat certain kinds of foods (usually not very nourishing ones!), or perhaps they will appear to eat almost nothing. Mealtimes are transformed into tense, anxious occasions when mothers will try all the tricks they know to persuade their offspring to eat. These may vary from tempting and cajoling, ignoring the uneaten meal, to becoming angry and insisting that the food is eaten. All may be to no avail. If a person refuses to eat, there is precious little that anyone else can do about it. Mothers feel alarmed, upset and often very rejected by their children's refusal to eat. Fortunately, in the process of ordinary development, such behaviour is usually short-lived.

The small child, having made her point, starts to eat normally again. But what point is she actually trying to make?

Assuming that the child is not unwell, she may simply be asserting that *she* and not her parents is in charge of nourishing herself. She is exercising a newly discovered sense of power. In the process of doing so, she learns that she can have a very controlling effect on her parents. She may revel in the attention she receives, and quite enjoy the mealtime battles which she is always able to win. Since this attention may reinforce the food-refusing habit rather than discourage it, parents might learn not to 'make too much of it', not to over-react and make the child the central focus of family attention.

Parents with a daughter in an anorexic phase sometimes receive the same sort of advice. But in truth, their situation is a very different one. When dealing with small children, we are accustomed to a certain degree of irrationality. We *know* that they will sometimes act things out rather than reason them out. This may be irritating, but it is not shocking. When a young adult, a girl of 14 or 15, someone with whom the parents have previously had a good and reasonable relationship, suddenly begins simply to refuse to eat, they are at a loss to know what to do. She denies that there are difficulties, says she *is* eating enough when clearly she is not and is inclined to angry outbursts if her parents 'nag' her about her eating. She begins to be deceitful, to lie with seeming ease about how much she eats. One mother told of her overwhelming disappointment when her daughter was found out deceiving the family with her 'egg trick'. The daughter, after several days of refusing to eat with the family, had reluctantly agreed to eat a boiled egg for her tea. On clearing away the tea things, the mother found that instead of eating her egg as she had appeared to do, the girl had pierced a hole in the bottom of the shell so that the yolk poured out into the egg-cup. She had eaten only the white of the egg – which of course does not contain many calories! The daughter normally cleared away the tea things and washed up. It was only because a telephone call interrupted the routine that the 'trick' was ever discovered.

The anorexic obsession with food often goes beyond the young woman's own eating. She takes a detailed interest in what other family members eat, and constantly urges them to eat more. I have known brothers, sisters and parents to develop their own weight problems for the first time under the ever-watchful and coercive persuasions of the anorexic family member. This obsessive desire to feed others springs partly from her constant preoccupation with food; she is preoccupied especially with foods which she denies herself. By preparing food for other people – and she particularly enjoys cooking fattening foods for them – she is partly satisfying her own need to be involved with food. She also needs the reassurance which comes from seeing that other people eat more than she does. She has lost touch with the actual minute quantities of food she consumes herself; every mouthful seems a vast amount. In order to be sure that she is eating less than 'normal', normal must be similarly magnified.

Perhaps even more horrifying for parents is the fact that their daughters appear to lose all touch with reality as far as their size and weight are concerned. Indeed, this is not merely an apparent loss; she really cannot measure herself by any objective standard. They try tactfully to point out to her that she is getting terribly thin; they ask in fear and trembling about her weight. They may be greeted with a tirade of abuse, or they may be gently reassured that everything is really under control and they are fussing about nothing. I have come across mothers who had been subjected for so long to this systematic bending of reality that they were in half a mind to believe that five stone two pounds really is a reasonable weight for a five-foot-three 15-year-old!

Some parents report that in addition to their daughter's bizarre behaviour about eating, she has also undergone something of a personality change. A number of girls who later become anorexic are, throughout their childhood years, pleasant, easy people, who get on well with their parents and who do not readily display anger and hostility. The advent of the symptoms about food actually gives them something to fight about. They change from being pleasant, compliant and cheerful youngsters to sulky, stubborn and often demanding young women. Later on in the chapter we shall see that this behaviour is sometimes long overdue. But for worried and confused parents, it just seems like a terrifying transformation.

Most of my initial enquiries about help and treatment come from mothers who are undergoing the ordeal of living with an anorexic daughter. They are often in a state of acute anxiety, both about how to manage the current situation and about their daughters' likely future. If the problem has been going on for a long time, they may also feel depressed themselves and drained of their own resources. One cannot but feel enormous sympathy for these troubled families in their struggle to survive and overcome their difficulties.

Family backgrounds

If the idea of 'a good family' has any meaning at all today, then it is certainly an idea we should apply to the sorts of families from which anorexics usually come.

Writers are in general agreement that not only are the families of anorexics usually materially quite comfortable, but they are normally very caring and concerned as well. Experiences of working with families with an anorexic member certainly support this generalisation. Without exception, the families we come across are families who take their responsibilities seriously and want the best for their children. This is true whether the child lives with one parent or two, and whether or not the family is structured in the traditional nuclear form.

Some writers, as we shall see, have suggested that anorexic women come from families who manifest certain sorts of psychopathology. We shall consider their views carefully, but first, a note of caution: the families who are seen in treatment when their daughters or sisters have already become anorexic are families under almost unbearable stress. Any observations about them and their behaviour must be evaluated in this light. Before we accept any of the so-called theories about the interaction in 'anorexic families', or before we agree with generalisations about the psychology of 'anorexic parents', we must ask ourselves, how could any family possibly behave normally if it lived with a woman who insists on systematically starving herself before their eyes? We shall see that professionals in the mental health field find it difficult enough to manage to maintain a consistent approach when they are working with anorexic women. For families I should say that it is quite impossible.

Before turning to some of the writers who have made a positive contribution to our understanding of anorexic women in the context of their families, I should like to illustrate just how unhelpful some approaches to the issue can be.

Peter Lambley[1] in his book *How to Survive Anorexia* paints a positively Dickensian picture of the parents of young women who go on to develop an anorexic condition. He portrays them as family-centred people who are very frightened of the outside world and who communicate this fear to their children. They are over-controlling in the extreme.

> If she does not please her parents, she will be sneered and jeered at. She fears this (justly) and cannot take it lightly because she knows that this is how they treat the outside world . . . It is the ultimate threat, the ultimate punishment held over the child and keeps her locked in her parents' world: 'Do it our way; please us or we will treat you as an outsider. And if you dare to persist in getting things wrong, we shall turn all our hostility on you – the hostility with which we treat outsiders; and worse, if you ever rebel or question us, we will really reject you.'[2]

He goes on to describe how dangerous these parents really are:

> Not only do they selectively neglect their children – over attending to them only in specific performance-orientated ways – but they really do reject their rebellious children emotionally . . . The parents were interested in their children only as long as they could have control. They seldom troubled themselves by visiting offspring who no longer lived in the home . . . To be blunt, we found that the parents of anorexics were capable of a high degree of cruelty and disinterest.[3]

Blunt, indeed. Finally, he accuses them of dishonesty.[4]

> Janet had always known that her parents were 'phoney' as she put
> it – one thing to the world at large and another at home . . .
> Anorexics are known to lie to themselves and to others endlessly.
> Thanks to Janet and others we now know where the ability comes
> from; they are taught it at home.

But Doctor Lambley does not elicit the information to support his hypothesis in the normal way – by talking with the families concerned and by listening to them. Rather, he persuades his confused clients to secretly tape record conversations with their parents which they then play back to him! (Remember, it is *he* who accuses *them* of dishonesty.)

The example which he uses to illustrate his novel approach to research is the family of a young woman he calls Janet. In the 'secret tape' made by Janet, he hears her mother suggesting that perhaps he is not a very good doctor. Janet's mother complains that Doctor Lambley has asked her questions about her marriage, suggesting to her that he believes her to be in some way responsible for Janet's difficulties. She insists that she would not do anything to hurt her daughter and that she wants only the best for her. Lambley seems to interpret this as proof of the mother's 'guilt'. If he approaches parents in the spirit in which he writes about them, I can well believe that they feel the need to defend themselves against his views.

He seems not to be prepared to work with families, but only against them. He seems to have convinced himself that he cares more about his anorexic clients than their parents do, an assumption which I personally find absurd. No. Common sense, coupled with a little experience of working with people, should be enough to convince us that if we approach a particular group of people full of presuppositions about their guilt, if we create ready-made culprits for ourselves, we lose forever the possibility of discovering anything approaching an understanding of them.

To repudiate the kind of approach which blames and vilifies families is not however to say that families are not sometimes a crucial element in the process of recovery. We need now to look at some of the major contributions to our understanding of the family context of anorexia.

Hilde Bruch[5] was the first writer to carefully and systematically investigate the kinds of families from which her anorexic patients came. She looked not only at the families in the present, but tried also to reconstruct the relationship between parents and children when the children were small. Her conclusions are, I think, extremely important and merit serious attention.

Bruch concluded that the mothers of women who later become anorexic had often been 'too good'. They had been very careful, very correct and perhaps over-anxious about their children's welfare. She relates this to the process of feeding. Bruch describes mothers who anticipated their child's needs. They instinctively 'knew', or thought they knew, what the child wanted and when, and met the need without the child having to 'ask'.

The distinguished paediatrician and psychoanalyst, Donald Winnicott, describes the same phenomenon, though not in relation to anorexia. He explains what can happen between the mother and the very young child when the mother seems to be almost 'too good'.[6]

> Mothers who have had several children begin to be so good at the technique of mothering that they do all the right things at the right moments, and then the infant who has begun to become separate from the mother has no means of gaining control of all the good things that are going on. The creative gesture, the cry, the protest, all the little signs that are supposed to produce what the mother does, all these things are missing, because the mother has already met the need just as if the infant were still merged with her and she with the infant. In this way the mother, by being a seemingly good mother, does something worse than castrate[7] the infant. The latter is left with two alternatives: either being in a state of permanent regression and of being merged with the mother, or else staging a total rejection of the mother, even of the seemingly good mother.

Winnicott's views on the problems of early childhood and infancy may seem at first sight to have little to do with anorexia. But the similarity between what he has observed in his work and what Hilde Bruch has to say about anorexia is quite striking.

Winnicott suggests that in the very early stages of life, mother and baby have a close, symbiotic relationship, in which the baby experiences the mother as an extension of herself. But, he believes, as the baby comes to experience herself as a separate person, the mother must be able to adapt to the baby's changing perceptions and move on from the state of being merged with the child, a state in which she has a profoundly intuitive understanding and anticipation of the baby's needs. If the mother continues to anticipate the child's needs without the child ever having to express them, that child will never learn that her behaviour brings her the response she wants. Babies need to learn that by crying they can gain their mother's attention and 'tell' her that they are hungry. If the baby is never allowed to express her need, she may grow into a very well-nourished baby but she will not have learned the important lesson that she has a voice and that this is a voice to which people will respond. This experience is fundamental to acquiring a sense of power, of ability to act on and in the world, rather than being a passive spectator. Further, the ability of the mother to allow the child to experience her separateness is essential for the baby to develop a sense of self and autonomy.

Winnicott[8] expresses surprise that so many mothers manage intuitively to get the process right. Without benefit of theory, most are able to let the child move from a state of being merged into one in which mother and baby are separate. Why do some run into problems? Prevailing fashions in child care have something to do with the process. The emphasis placed by professional experts on schedules and routines, so popular in the 1950s and which still play a part in the thinking of some maternity hospitals today, positively discourages mothers from really responding to their baby's needs. If child care is seen as an activity to be based around the book and the clock, then the wants of the baby are probably the last things the mother has time to think about. Bruch[9] suggests that infants who later go on to become anorexic youngsters may never have really learned to respond to the needs of their *own* bodies. The child never has a chance to get hungry because mother always feeds her before she gets hungry. The child learns that feeding has something to do with her relationship with her mother, something which mother decides upon and which is not connected with meeting her own bodily need for food. Bruch believes that the difficulties which anorexics have in identifying bodily sensations, and in particular hunger, are related to a failure in this very early learning process.

As she describes it, this process continues, and the young girl goes on satisfying her parents' needs at the expense of her own. She grows into a compliant, pleasant and rather unquestioning youngster, who always seems to do what other people approve of. She is usually very reasonable, very grown-up in her approach to life and does not upset or disappoint her parents in any way. What she fails to do is to develop a sense of her own worth as an independent person who is able to take control of her own life. The young woman who has developed (or rather failed to develop) in this way will experience difficulties at adolescence. When she reaches the point in her life at which independence and autonomy are required, she is likely to feel unable to cope with the demands which are made upon her. If we consider again Winnicott's ideas about mothers who continue to behave as though they and their children were one rather than two separate individuals, we might expect such children to have serious difficulties in separating from their families. We shall return to this point later, when we examine the crucial relationship between mothers and daughters which is such a powerful feature of anorexia.

Salvador Minuchin is a family therapist who has studied anorexia within the context of family interaction.[10] He is less interested in past relationships and histories of the problem and focuses directly upon the actual interaction between family members in the here-and-now. He describes work with anorexics in the very young age group (9–16). He concludes that the families from which anorexics come are usually 'enmeshed', that is, over-involved with one another, where space for individual growth and difference is very limited. This is quite consistent with Hilde Bruch's findings about passivity and lack of a real identity in the clients she works with. Minuchin also finds that the families with whom he works tend to avoid conflict. Differences of opinion are concealed and often quite painful and unhappy situations between family members are denied.

Minuchin works with the family both to relieve the initial symptoms of food refusal, using the 'family lunch session', and to enable them to resolve and alter some of their interactional patterns in the longer term. When working with very young people who have recently developed an anorexic symptom, this would seem a very sensible approach. However, Minuchin's methods appeal to some people and not to others. Sheila MacLeod[11] offers a characteristically elegant account of her own responses to his work. 'Perhaps I am being insularly British', she says, 'in finding such a carry-on typically American in its crassness.' Perhaps she is. But she will not be alone in her views and her chapter on the various treatment approaches is essential reading.

I am often asked by parents and by anorexic women themselves whether they should engage in therapy for the family or whether individual therapy for the anorexic member is 'best'. I can only say 'it all depends . . .'.

It depends particularly on the circumstances of the anorexic episode. If the young woman is *very* young, is living with her family and has very limited scope because of her age for making changes in her life, then clearly, most therapists would want, at least initially, to involve the family. Whether they would continue to do so would depend upon the response of the individual and the family to that form of help. Equally, if the woman were in her early thirties, had not lived with her parents for a decade or so and had developed her anorexic symptom some time after she had left the family, then probably most therapists would begin with individual treatment and only include the family of origin if this was felt to be useful. One kind of treatment does not rule out another. In Minuchin's case of the Kaplan family,[12] the anorexic in the family was seen by Minuchin for a number of years after the family therapy had ceased.

There is only one rule. That is that all situations in which anorexic symptoms arise are different. There are common elements, which include the difficulty of an individual in achieving and maintaining a sense of herself as a free and autonomous person. Sometimes families are crucially involved in this difficulty, sometimes they are not. If we work from situations rather than ready-made theories, we are likely not to go too far wrong.

I want to turn now to the feature of the family lives of anorexic women which I find most characteristic: the mother/daughter relationship. I can say with certainty that I have never worked with an anorexic woman who had a 'straightforward' relationship with her mother.

That is not to say that young women who go through an anorexic experience have *bad* relationships with their mothers (although some of them do), but simply that the relationships are normally complex and puzzling to both mother and daughter.

You may find that recovery from anorexia does involve some work on and changes in this relationship. But it is often one of the hardest issues for the young woman to face. I want therefore to describe the kinds of relationships between mothers and daughters which I have come across, in the hope that some mothers and daughters will be able to identify with what they read. The kind of relationship I have in mind is one which is characterised by ambivalence (the simultaneous coexistence of both strong positive and negative feelings), and by difficulties about separateness and differentiation.

As we have already suggested, there is a sense in which we might have guessed that the symptom of anorexia would point us in the direction of the relationship with the mother. Feeding and being nourished is essentially an activity which goes on between mothers and children. A disorder of eating is therefore likely to be associated with difficulties in this relationship.

I am not suggesting however, that difficulties between mothers and daughters *cause* anorexia. Rather, I am inclined to see the difficulties as symptomatic of the regression into a state of child-like dependence which characterises anorexia. If anorexia is a symptom of a retreat from independence, where better to retreat to than back to mother?

But we cannot leave the matter there. The final section of this chapter is an attempt to view the relationship between anorexic daughters and their mothers in the context of what we know in general about mother/daughter relationships in our society. My contention is that what we see manifest in the regressive relationship of the anorexic to her mother we may also find latent in many if not most mother/daughter relationships as they currently exist.

One of the most striking features of working with young anorexic women is the observation of how central a person mother is to them.

They frequently assert that the most important person in their lives is their mother. Where they do not say so, they often indicate that this is the case by the amount of time they spend talking about her.

There is sometimes a tendency to idealise the relationship with the mother. 'What I really enjoy is going shopping with mummy. Just the two of us. We have such similar tastes in things. We're really more like sisters.' 'My mother is the only one who really understands me. I know she's the only one who can help me with this problem.'

But when the subject is pursued, often, just below the surface are feelings of deprivation, of not getting enough of mother. 'She's always so tired and busy with the others to look after and the house. We hardly ever get time to really talk any more. Sometimes we sit up late together at night. She's the only person who really knows what it's like for me.'

This feeling of not getting enough of mother's time, attention and caring can lead to resentments against other members of the family. 'She spends a whole day a week with Gillian [an older daughter-in-law with a small baby] and then hasn't got time for anything else. Gillian's got John. She doesn't *need* mum like I do.'

A few anorexic women are strongly attached to their fathers, although this is quite rare. Where it is the case, there are often feelings of guilt that father is closer to her than he is to mother, or resentment that mother does not show more interest in her. More often I find that fathers are somewhat distant figures: which in itself is not unusual in our contemporary families, whether nuclear or not. However, it has become apparent that women who develop anorexia tend to be very *interested* in their fathers. Sometimes this interest is positive and takes the form of a longing to please and be close to; in other instances, it takes a negative form and may even constitute a kind of loathing. But the interest is always there. Fathers do seem to be mysterious figures. Sometimes feared, sometimes adored – but objects of fascination who are largely unknown.

In spite of the presence of the 'unreal' father, a great many anorexic girls *behave* as though they and their mothers were in fact the only two members of the family. Everyone else is felt to have little or nothing to offer and may be seen as a positive nuisance because of the demands they make on mother's time.

Wherever possible, I try to see mothers alone at least once, though never without the permission of the daughter. At first, this is often resisted by the daughter: any suggestion that they are two separate people with different points of view may be much too frightening at this stage. When I succeed in seeing the mother, I usually get a very different picture from the rather idealised one which the woman with the anorexic disorder has painted. 'I really want to help her so much. But honestly, I just can't take any more. She wants my constant attention. All the time. That's why I gave up my job. Of course, I didn't tell her that.'

I have worked with two young women who insisted that the only way they could eat was to go out to restaurants with their mothers, leaving the rest of the family at home. In one case, this was a daily occurrence. Both mothers complained of how stressful this was in terms of both time and money. One of them had also to prepare and leave a meal for the rest of the family. One of the daughters insisted that her mother really enjoyed their meals out together, that it got her out of the house. The other simply said that she could not survive any other way. It is interesting that in spite of their protests, the mothers concerned still did as their daughters asked and could not find a way of resisting the demands. These mothers still felt responsible for their daughters' nutrition, even though both were young adults and one of them had lived away from home for a year or more.

Other mothers describe the strain they feel from their daughters' endless rituals around food, the pressure which is exerted on them to eat with her, or to eat large meals while she starves herself. The 'talks' so valued by the anorexic woman are often experienced by her mother as painful and circular, leading nowhere.

To summarise: the anorexic and her mother would, typically, both agree that they are very 'close'. The daughter feels a great need for her mother and usually anger that she is not getting her needs met. The mother on the other hand, feels as though she is doing everything she can, but in effect she is powerless to help. She too feels angry and frustrated that it never seems to be enough, even though she may neglect the rest of her family in her efforts to help. Her powerlessness in the face of her daughter's difficulties can make her feel guilty and failed.

The reality of the interaction between them is often different again. I have found mothers to be quite frightened of their daughters. With the wretched threat of the daughters not eating hanging over them, they experience a kind of tyranny: they tend to agree with their daughters when they do not really mean it because they are frightened that the slightest hint of disagreement will bring tears and 'make her worse'.

If we take a step back, we might want to say that this sort of relationship is in many ways characteristic of that which exists between a mother and a much younger child. The closeness between the two of them, the feeling that they alone understand each other, the bitter resentments and rages on both sides, seem to indicate that they are not in fact existing as two separate individuals. It is as though the daughter believes that she depends for her very survival upon her mother. And the mother behaves as though this were the case. Mother may protest, she may tell her daughter that she should take more responsibility for herself, but her behaviour belies her words; her daughter is still her mother's responsibility and not her own. The daughter believes that mother understands her better than she understands herself. The mother continues to have a close and empathic perception of her daughter's needs, a perception which may be accurate, but which is nevertheless inappropriate when it occurs between two adults. It is as though both expect too much of each other and of the relationship. The daughter behaves as though she needs total care – as a tiny infant may do – and the mother consents to a kind of union with her daughter which amounts to a life's work.

Mothers are often so involved with their daughters that they really experience their daughters' distress as their own. Sometimes in interviews with anorexic girls and their mothers, I am unable to tell whose feelings are being described. 'The days seem so long,' one mother said. 'We just go from one awful mealtime to the next.' Her daughter looked upset, as though she might cry. Mother really was speaking for them both.

So far, I have been talking about women who have developed an anorexic disorder and the kinds of relationships they have with their mothers. The picture I have painted may sound to some quite bizarre, pathological even. The behaviour indeed may be unusual, but I want to go on to suggest that the *feelings* which accompany the behaviour are very common indeed in our society. Jane Flax,[13] a psychotherapist whose clinical experience is not with anorexic women but with college students with a variety of difficulties, believes that the need for nurturing together with independence is a cause of conflict in the lives of many women. She says, 'What women want is an experience of both nurturance and autonomy within an intimate relationship. What makes this wish so strong and, for many women, so unattainable, is that psychological development occurs within the patriarchal family – in which the mother is the primary nurturer and the father is the symbol of authority.'

She goes on to explain how this situation which we generally take for granted affects the relationships which mothers are able to form with their daughters. She suggests that the difficulties have their origins in the mother's closer identification with her girl children. By virtue of the fact that they are both female, the mother is likely to see the girl child as 'herself' whereas the boy is clearly and from the start an 'other'. Because of this closer identification, mothering girls is likely to stir up more unresolved conflict in the mother. Flax goes on to say, 'Women often admit that themselves. With girl children, the confusion over who is the child and who is the mother is intensified. Women patients have reported to me that they often felt pressure from their own mothers to provide the care the mothers themselves had lacked in their childhood. Women are less likely to have these confusions or expectations aroused with boy children because men are not seen as nurturers in our culture.'

She suggests that mothers may also have an unconscious difficulty about physical closeness with their daughters. The strong social prohibitive against physical love between members of the same sex has more serious consequences for girls than it does for boys. Men are able to rediscover with a woman the physical closeness and nurturing they once had with their mothers. As Jane Flax puts it, 'As adults, women must repress yearnings for physical closeness with other women so that once the mother's body is lost through differentiation, it is supposed to be lost forever; but a boy can replace his mother with another female.'

Finally, we have to acknowledge that mothers may unconsciously feel afraid to give their daughters too much nurturing; they know only too well that the daughter will have to learn to nurture other people and may very well not ever have her own needs met.

What then are the results of this conflict which Flax believes to be inherent in the way mothers feel about their daughters?

> As a result of all these conflicts, it is more difficult for the mother to be as emotionally available as her infant daughter needs her to be. Women are therefore more likely to retain a wish to return to the infantile state . . . If the symbiotic experience has not been adequate, the process of separation and individuation that follows is also more difficult for the female infant. She lacks to some extent the firm base from which to differentiate . . . If symbiosis has not been adequate, this phase will either be delayed or premature, as the infant desperately attempts to assert some autonomy without the inner resources to do so. In either case, the sense of self and ability to form relations with others are likely to be more fragile and impaired.[14]

We must remind ourselves that this analysis refers to relationships between mothers and daughters *in general*. It is not an account of the origins of anorexia. Yet when we look back on what has already been said about the peculiarly intense but unsatisfying relationships which anorexic women and their mothers tend to have, a few pieces of the jigsaw seem to begin to make a new pattern.

The feeling of never getting enough nurturing, never getting enough of mother, which is such a common feature of an anorexic phase, now appears to be much more widespread. A lot of women, it seems, share it. The ambivalence which I have described on the part of mothers with an anorexic daughter, wanting to continue to nurture them but feeling both worried about their lack of autonomy and tyrannised by their demands, now seems as though it might be a feature of many mother/daughter relationships.

What we find in women with an anorexic disorder though, is a much clearer expression of these conflicts. By way of explanation, we can either suggest that the conflict in the relationships between anorexics and their mothers is actually more acute than it is between 'normal' mothers and daughters, or that it is simply more sharply and clearly expressed. Both of course may be true, but I suspect that what we are really seeing is a disturbing *manifestation* of a relationship which in our sort of society will always be problematic.

Why does the anorexic woman begin to show and express the unresolvable needs she has for being nurtured, the bottomless pit of emptiness inside herself which she feels can only be filled by more and more of mother? The answer I think is that a woman in an anorexic phase has temporarily given up trying to pretend to be independent. The struggle to make sense of life as an autonomous adult has been abandoned. All her child-like feelings and needs come flooding back. If there is a mother in the picture, she is bound to become a target for these confused and ambivalent feelings. If there is no mother, it may be a husband, sister, friend who finds him/herself the recipient of demands for nurturing which seem impossible to meet.

Paradoxically, while her soul cries out for nurturing and care, she resolutely refuses to nurture her body, even in the most minimal way, and she rejects anyone else's attempts to do it for her. Here we have stumbled upon another of the startling dynamics of anorexia, one which makes it at once both difficult to treat, but treatable. The need to be cared for, looked after, to be almost totally dependent and the desire to be autonomous, separate, isolated even, produce a conflict which it is impossible for the woman to live at peace with.

No family is an island

This chapter has been a difficult one to write. By now, some of the difficulties will have become apparent.

Whatever research we are able to accumulate on the families which 'produce' anorexia, however shrewd our observations might become of the relationships which exist between anorexic women and the people who are close to them, we are still looking at an essentially social phenomenon.

Families do not create themselves. They are more than 'interlocking networks of relationships'. The family is the basic and fundamental social and economic unit of our society. As such, it has a variety of social functions to perform. These include providing for the social and material well-being of children. They also include teaching children how to become adults. As we saw in Chapter 2, we live in the kind of world which is itself riven with conflicts about what adult women should be like. If families unconsciously mediate these conflicts to their young women, we should not be surprised – indeed we would be surprised if they did not.

Any theory of anorexia which starts and ends with an analysis of families is mistaken. The problem of thousands of gifted young women every year starving themselves to the point of death will never be solved by simply working with their families. That is only one dimension of the issue. In some instances however, it is an important dimension. Families may not be the ones to create the problems but certainly, they are sometimes able to provide the arena in which they can be resolved.

5
The Ideal Weight: A Common Approach to Treatment

If you are in an anorexic phase, the decision to look for help with your difficulties is a very crucial and serious one. You may feel very frightened indeed at the prospect of letting anyone know how bad you feel, and scared too that your treatment will be taken out of your own hands.

In this chapter I want to look at what the aims of treatment should be, and to describe some of the approaches which are often used. It is very important that you, as someone who may be on the receiving end of treatment, understand what issues are involved, so that you can make active decisions about what happens to you. It is also important for you to understand that people who work in the helping professions are human too, and that your own distress will have an effect on them.

If you are going to recover successfully from your anorexic episode, your treatment must have two aims. One is to safeguard your physical well-being, to ensure that you survive. The other is to enable you to come to some understanding of the issues underlying the difficulties with food, and to develop different solutions to them. Most recent writers on the subject of anorexia agree that both of these aims are vitally necessary for successful recovery. There are however wide areas of disagreement about the relationship between one and the other and about the relative importance of weight increase as opposed to understanding and change in attitude.

Before looking briefly at what some other writers have to say on the subject, it should be made quite clear that during an anorexic phase you can become physically very ill, and even that you can die. All of us who work with anorexic women want to help you to prevent that from happening. If you reach a point where you can no longer maintain a minimal level of physical health, then you need first aid. No therapist, however talented or experienced, can or should attempt to work with a dying woman. This, of course, does not mean that weight gain is in itself any sort of solution to your real problems. On the contrary. You may find that in the early stages of recovery, weight gain is a very poor guide to the progress you are actually making in learning to deal with your life in a more satisfactory way.

Hilde Bruch, in *The Golden Cage*,[1] suggests that in addition to the life-threatening effects of severe and prolonged starvation, women who are very severely emaciated may not be able to progress in their understanding because their thinking is impaired. She suggests that a weight of 90–95 lbs is the minimum necessary for a woman to be able to function well enough to use psychotherapy. She does not however lay down any hard and fast rules about 'target weights' or 'ideal weights'. She is merely asserting that women should be physically well enough to be able to work at their problems. This seems to me to be a basically sensible approach. It leaves the woman and her helper free to negotiate and decide about the amount of weight, if any, which the woman initially needs to gain.

The idea of a target or ideal weight has gained a certain amount of popularity in recent years. R.L. Palmer[2] advocates that the doctor should set as a target the average or 'normal' weight for the woman's size, whether she is seen for treatment in an in-patient or out-patient context. A. H. Crisp[3] suggests that the woman with an anorexic disorder should reach the weight she held before she entered the anorexic phase. This he regards as a prerequisite to recovery. He is suggesting that the woman will not begin to re-experience the conflicts which led her to adopt an anorexic solution until after she has achieved the weight which went with the original conflicts. I find this a very interesting idea. The problem with it is that it attributes too much importance to weight itself. It is making a fundamentally 'anorexic' mistake; it treats weight as a magical quality, allowing numbers on the dial to take over from reality. This is really the difficulty with all approaches to treatment which lay down rigid rules about weight gain. As Hilde Bruch says,[4] 'The patient needs to be instructed, and also the family, that in spite of outer appearances, this is not an illness of weight and appetite – the essential problem relates to inner doubts and lack of self-confidence.'

It must be said again, gaining weight, although it may sometimes be necessary to ensure survival, is no solution at all to the problem of anorexia. Most writers on the subject agree that it is at best a partial and temporary measure.

The experience of treatment

In spite of the insistence of most contemporary writers on anorexia that psychotherapy is vitally necessary as part of the treatment approach, the most common complaint made by anorexics and their families about the treatment they have received, is that the focus has been almost exclusively on weight gain. 'He's not interested in me at all – just whether this old sack [indicating her body] weighs seven stone three or seven stone four.'

Hilde Bruch[5] believes that where hospitalisation is necessary, it is best carried out in special units where the staff are qualified and experienced in the work. The fact remains that the vast majority of women with an anorexic disorder are not treated in such units. It is therefore very difficult to generalise about 'standard' forms of treatment. My own account is necessarily impressionistic; it is based on what I have heard from several hundred women, in interviews and letters.

Anorexia is not always treated in psychiatric settings. Since the general practitioner is normally the first helper to whom the woman is referred, it is up to her (or him) as to where or whether the woman is referred for more specialist help.

Quite a number of general practitioners do initially try to handle the problem themselves on an out-patient basis. This is particularly likely to be the case where the doctor has known the woman or her family for some time and frankly sometimes cannot believe that the sensible girl she knew now needs specialist care.

Such treatment by a general practitioner or college medical service can sometimes be very successful. Over-reaction to the problem can, as we shall see, be disastrous. If the difficulties have not been going on for too long and if the woman is able to seek help for herself at an early stage, the outcome is likely to be good in any case. She may be able to help herself with encouragement and some superficial discussion of her difficulties.

Where help from the general practitioner is not sufficient, this is usually due to either the fact that the problem has gone too far – the symptoms were too severe – or that the doctor simply did not have the time. Counselling anorexic women *is* time-consuming; it is not surprising that many 'front line' health care workers are unable to take it on.

If you are referred to a specialist service, this may be to a psychiatrist, to a general physician or occasionally to a gynaecologist. The latter type of referral may be made if the initial anxiety is about the loss of menstruation. The general practitioner is likely to refer you to someone she knows, someone she believes to have an interest in the problem or to someone she has worked with before. The availability of specialist help obviously varies from one location to another. We therefore have the rather odd situation in which there is no single accepted referral 'route' for the woman believed to be suffering from anorexia.

But the outcome in terms of the kind of treatment you may receive may not, after all, turn out to be very different.

In 1874, William Gull[6] advised the following plan of treatment. 'The patients should be fed at regular intervals, and surrounded by persons who could have moral control over them, relations and friends being generally the worst attendants.' It is difficult to believe that over a century has gone by with so little improvement in the treatment which many anorexics are now offered.

Here is Heather's experience. It is typical of the experiences of dozens of women seen in counselling.

Heather, a quiet, pretty girl from a city in the north of England, began to lose weight while she was studying for her A-levels. After leaving school she spent some months in Italy before going to take up a college place in the south. Whilst abroad, she gained some weight. The first term at college was a strain. Heather missed home, she did not make friends very easily and felt that her peers were much more sophisticated than she, her northern accent sounded out of place and her rather homeloving interests now seemed dull. She resolved to lose the weight she had gained. By the time the Christmas vacation came round, she had lost a stone and a half and weighed about seven stones. Heather somehow limped on for a further two terms. Her college tutor became concerned and she was referred to the college medical service. She begged to be allowed to carry on until the end of the year when she could have the long summer vacation at home and gain some weight. She just managed to pass her end of year exams and arrived home weighing five-and-a-half stones. Her parents were horrified, took her to the family doctor and she was admitted to the local general hospital. She was told she would have to reach a weight of eight stones. Confused and terrified, Heather submitted to a regime of bed-rest and a high calorie diet. By the end of August she had reached a weight of just over seven stones and was discharged from hospital, feeling massively bloated and fat. She was seen once as an out-patient before returning south to take up her college place and to commence her second year.

By Christmas, her weight had again dropped to just above six stones. The college medical service was quicker off the mark this time; she was admitted to the psychiatric hospital which served the college catchment area. This time, there was talk of a 'contract'. But according to Heather, as she remembers the experience, she was given no say at all in what her treatment would be. A 'target weight' of eight stones was once again set. This time Heather was told she would not be allowed out of bed until she had gained a stone and a half. All privileges, such as having books to read, a television to watch, people to talk to, were dependent on how much weight she gained. She had no choice at all of the kinds of foods she ate. By this time acutely depressed, Heather ate nothing for a week. In an effort to modify her stubborn behaviour, even her pillows were taken away and she was not allowed to sit up. The nurses were instructed not to talk to her at all if she did not eat her meals. She wanted to write to her parents. Paper and pen were withheld. Finally, of course, Heather began to eat. She gained weight quite rapidly as the amounts of food she had to consume were very large. If she refused any food, she once again lost the 'luxuries' (like visitors) which she had earned. By March, her weight had reached seven-and-a-half stones. Her parents discharged her and took her home. The hospital thought she had done 'very well', but advised a longer stay to put on the full amount of the 'ideal' weight. After two weeks at home, Heather took an overdose of her mother's sleeping pills. This time she was admitted to a local psychiatric hospital near to her parents' home. Here at last, she found people to talk to. She was very depressed, felt humiliated and beaten. In addition, her eating had gone entirely out of control. She over-ate constantly and developed the self-destructive habit of making herself sick in order to control her weight.

It took Heather several years of hard work in therapy and constant anxiety about her weight to achieve sufficient self-confidence for life to become anything near to normal again.

Heather's second experience of hospitalisation was a particularly brutal and unhelpful one. It is not however, untypical. The technique of withdrawing all 'privileges' to enforce weight gain is known as behaviour modification. It enjoyed something of a vogue in the 1970s and is still quite widely used today. It is an attempt to reinforce eating by rewarding it. In the very short term, of course, it works. Anorexic women, like anyone else, can be induced to do what they do not want to do by making the alternative so unpleasant that they really have no choice.

The cost however, can be enormous. As early as 1974, Hilde Bruch wrote a paper drawing attention to the dangers of such an approach.[7] She suggests that rapid weight gain without any attention to the underlying difficulties can lead to suicidal depression.

If we return to the internal conflicts experienced by the anorexic woman, it is not difficult to understand why such an approach is so destructive. I have suggested that anorexia represents an attempt to maintain control. It is a symptom of the fact that the woman regards her life as generally being out of her control. Limiting her food intake and continuing to lose weight are the only things she really feels able to do. She feels part of herself to be 'strong', 'good' and 'worthwhile'. This is the part which is able to maintain control of her weight and which refuses to succumb to the temptation to be weak and to eat. Enforcing weight gain has the effect of dragging her out of that safe haven; the only aspect of life to which she can really feel committed is taken away. The sense of loss is bound to be vast.

If the woman in an anorexic phase has no sense of her own value, if she feels not only powerless, but worthless, it is only a precarious sense of her own worth she maintains by staying very thin. She feels that at any moment she might lose her ability to continue the struggle. The real temptation to *eat* is sometimes almost overwhelming. (It is only after recovery that anorexic women are able to express how physically and emotionally painful starvation is; at the time they tend to deny that they have an appetite.)

So an approach to treatment which focuses on weight gain as a route to recovery must have the effect of making the woman feel an utter failure. As well as loathing her new fat body, she will interpret it as a sign of her own weakness and stupidity.

If we understand anorexia as a problem which has to do with control, and if we see the long-term aims of treatment as enabling the woman to take a proper and reasonable control of her own life, to become an effective agent in her own affairs, then surely any approach which begins by taking away the final vestiges of her attempts to control her life must be at best unhelpful, and at worst, downright dangerous.

When you initially come for treatment with an anorexic symptom, you may find that you have an ambivalent attitude towards your own difficulties. Part of you really wants help. You may feel desperate and sick of the continual struggle against food. You probably want relief. You are certainly quite sensible enough to see that the relentless path you are pursuing will lead nowhere. On the other hand, you may not feel in the least able or prepared to give up the struggle and to attempt to come to terms with your difficulties from the point of view of a normal weight. You may not be able to envisage how this could be possible. It is unthinkable. The anorexic woman will sometimes present one side of this ambivalent picture: 'I really want to get well. I know I've got to stop doing this. I'm going to eat properly from now on.' Sometimes she will present the other. 'There's no way anyone is going to get me fat. There's nothing wrong with me. I know how I feel and they're all worrying about nothing.'

In the following chapter we will consider how to approach this ambivalence in the counselling situation. As far as refeeding is concerned, the people involved in inducing weight gain tend to ally themselves with one aspect of the woman's experience. They tell her that the part of her which wants to be 'well' is the good, healthy part. The part of her which obstinately clings to the anorexic solution is ill or bad or stupid. The very part of her experience which needs to be understood and which is crying out for help, the part of her which sees staying thin as the only possible way of going on living, is negated, ignored and labelled sick.

Thus it can and frequently does happen that when an anorexic woman is treated in hospital, her body becomes the object of struggle and confrontation between herself and those who are trying to 'treat' her. Their insistence that she gain weight elicits from her the response that she will not. Her stubbornness, for this is how it is often perceived, will in turn, help to renew their vigorous attempts to overcome it. She feels assaulted, mistreated and misunderstood and will resort to lying and deceit in her attempts to avoid giving in to them. When women recover from an anorexic episode, they often look back on this time with shame. 'I came out of hospital a much worse person than I went in.' 'Hospital? I learnt a lot of tricks there.'

Women suffering from anorexia are not dishonest or deceitful people. But if they experience their very existence to be in peril they will do anything within their power to try to survive. This is a healthy response, not a 'crazy' one. And hospital staff can of course be deceitful too. How often are anorexics not told that high calorie additives have been put into their food? Little wonder that they become suspicious of everything they eat.

In training sessions for nurses working with anorexic women, someone will often say at the end of the session, 'I certainly understand the problem better, but when I'm trying to get the patient to eat, if I show her any understanding, she will use it as an excuse not to eat.' On closer analysis, it is generally found to be the case that the nurse herself, as she develops a better understanding of how her patient feels, is less inclined to try to force her to eat with quite such vigour. She therefore feels as though she is failing as a nurse.

It might be relevant to ask whether in fact it is the prescribed regime which is failing. If nurses can only work well by being automata, if their sympathy and real insight into their patient's distress make them do a bad job, then surely we must be asking them to do the wrong job.

Nursing women with anorexia certainly is a very difficult job. omen in an anorexic phase evoke strong responses from their helpers which range all the way from horror to envy. This was brought home to me when I watched two nurses walking away from the bed of a young anorexic girl after 'lunch'. They had spent the best part of an hour trying to persuade her to eat. They had chatted with her, trying to divert her attention from the food she was eating, spoon-fed her in turns, told her what a stupid girl she was and finally walked away in defeat. As they walked back to the office together, one said to the other, 'Oh, I *wish* I had that kind of will-power. I've been doing quite well with my diet, but I had a real binge last night.' The nurse's response was a very natural and 'human' one. However, if her feelings were communicated in an unspoken way to the anorexic woman (and they will almost certainly have been picked up), then the nurse's demands will have appeared even more confusing to her. Anorexics make their helpers feel fat and frumpy. If these feelings are to be contained, worked through and not allowed to distort the work with the 'patient', then nurses, doctors, counsellors and anyone else concerned in the helping process will need adequate opportunity to explore and monitor their own feelings in relation to the problem. I myself always find that working with anorexic women makes me feel hungry. It is nothing new; it has been with me right from the start. I can only account for it by assuming that I would really like to eat for them.

If refeeding is necessary – and it by no means always is – then it should be approached with caution, with understanding and with an attitude of regret. It is straightforwardly dishonest to let anorexic women or their parents believe that feeding them up will solve any of the difficulties. It may on occasion and regretfully be necessary in order for the anorexic woman to engage in the real work of understanding herself and her own situation.

If a woman needs to be hospitalised for nutritional first aid, every attempt should be made to enhance rather than to reduce her sense of self-esteem. She should be encouraged to take as much control as she is able in deciding what is to happen to her. If hospitalisation is approached in a more compassionate and in a more individualised way, the woman will not gain so much weight in such a short time, she will be a more 'difficult' patient, she will need to be listened to as well as fed. But the chances of her being severely damaged in the process will hopefully be lessened.

Responses to hospitalisation

Hospital treatment obviously sometimes works. The woman recovers not only her weight, but also her sense of self, her sense of worth and her capacity to continue to grow rather than to shrink back into her anorexic half life. When it works, it is usually because the treatment is humane and balanced. Physical care is combined with therapeutic help and the woman's real needs are understood. But I will concentrate on the examples of hospitalisation which can prove to be less successful and helpful, because this is, frankly, what I most often come across. The majority of clients seen by myself and colleagues over a two-year period in a voluntary counselling agency for anorexics had already had at least one experience of hospitalisation. Many had spent months of their lives undergoing various hospital regimes. Most were re-referred for help because they had again lost weight. And this is the most pragmatic reason of all for considering much hospital treatment to be inadequate – it simply does not work in the long term. Until and unless the woman is ready and able to give up her anorexic life, weight is gained only to be lost again.

There are however reasons for believing that hospitalisation can sometimes not only fail to provide long-term help for the problem but that it can actually complicate and impede the process of recovery; it can make it much more difficult for women to deal with their real difficulties at a later stage.

Not all women respond to hospitalisation in the same way. Some actively resist the treatment they receive in hospital. They are 'uncooperative' and only finally consent to gain weight in order to be released and to once again pursue the goal of ultimate thinness. They literally eat their way out of hospital. They may pretend to comply with the aims of the hospital staff, but for these women it really is no more than a pretence; they know that the goal they have in mind is quite different. For some of these women, the experience of hospitalisation merely reinforces their own belief that no one understands them or is sympathetic to their secret obsession. The only way they can continue is by attempting to elude the doctors and carry on with a private regime of their own. Women in this position sometimes report that they will go for the statutory out-patient appointment after having drunk several pints of water. This will prove that they are maintaining their weight. Some have even reported that they put lead weights in their pockets before the ritual of weighing at the doctor's surgery. Suspicious doctors then sometimes respond by asking the woman to strip before being weighed. But really, this battle of wills, this attempt by the patient to outwit the doctor and her (or his) attempt to do the same in return, is utterly counter-productive. Women who have received this kind of 'help' are often deeply suspicious of anyone who attempts to talk with them about the problem in the future. They have learnt that help consists of an effort on the part of the helper to control their behaviour. Help appears to have nothing to offer these women themselves. This means that any kind of counselling or therapeutic help which may be offered at a later stage will be viewed with deep suspicion and the clients concerned may have the fear that all the counsellor really wants to do is to put them in the nearest hospital bed and fatten them up!

Women who have had bad experiences of hospitalisation in the past and have resisted them are also inclined to try to engage their helpers in a battle for control – even if the aim of the helper is to enable the woman to take control of her own life. She may fear that by agreeing with a single thing the counsellor says, she will be giving in and surrendering herself to someone else's will.

Other women who are hospitalised during an anorexic phase 'give in' very easily. It seems that whatever the hospital regime dictates, the woman will accept it and assume that it is sensible and right. This means that she is accepting the hospital's definition of her own behaviour – that it is stupid and rather childish and wrong. Given the very low self-esteem which young women have of themselves when they enter into an anorexic episode, it is often very easy to convince them that they are indeed stupid and wrong-headed. One of the central elements in anorexia is the tendency to want to please and to comply with other people's expectations. It is when complying and pleasing others becomes incompatible with the demands of real maturity and autonomy that anorexia tends to occur. It is the failure to take into account the real needs of the self and to clearly differentiate these from the needs of others which heralds the onset of the rebellious symptom in the first place. The young women who comply readily with a refeeding programme and deny their own inner conflicts about doing so, are really replacing an anorexic solution with another one which is all too similar. They are denying their own feelings about gaining weight and are going along with what they are told is sensible. They therefore come to mistrust their own feelings about food and weight and to regard them as entirely worthless; silly things which need to be buried and forgotten. In truth, they are issues which need to be acknowledged and worked through in relation to other aspects of women's lives.

There is yet another reason for regarding with some suspicion anorexic women who learn to go along with hospital expectations. Under pressure to eat large quantities of food, a number of women find that their anorexic symptoms give way to those of bulimia. In a recent group established for women who specifically wanted to work on the problem of over-eating and making themselves sick, we discovered that out of a group of nine women, seven had previously been hospitalised for anorexia. All had complied with a rigid feeding regime but had done so at the cost of not really learning and understanding what their own needs were in relation to food. They had begun to eat large quantities of food before they had come to terms with some of the real issues about control and independence. They fared quite well in hospital, where food intake was controlled by other people, but on discharge, found themselves unable to take decisions about their own nutritional needs. They therefore fell into the trap of continuing to eat everything which presented itself to them. But of course, they still felt controlled by the old anorexic obsession with thinness; to gain weight still felt ugly, slothful and disgusting. What choice then when eating has gone entirely out of control, but to try to control weight by any means available?

With these women, the emphasis on weight gain had not in any sense diminished their anorexic convictions. Rather it had reinforced the feelings of hopelessness and rejection. It had forced a compliance with other people's ideas of health and had led the women into deeper and deeper difficulties. The feelings of women in such a situation must be taken extremely seriously. To feel out of control of food and of feelings is terrifying. Self-harm, including attempts at suicide, is not uncommon.

Mention must be made of the role of parents in the process of hospitalisation. For parents, this can be one of the most painful and difficult aspects of the whole problem. Parents (mothers), more than anyone else, can see that their daughters are in need of help. If outsiders sometimes feel shocked, and horrified at the sight of an emaciated anorexic woman, for their mothers the sight is almost unbearable.

Consequently, parents are often initially in favour of their daughters going into hospital. Here, at least, their lives will be safe and help for the confusing tangle of feelings which exist can perhaps be offered. On the other hand, parents have to bear the brunt of their daughter's protests about the prospect of hospitalisation. They are very often the ones who have to apply the pressure to make her do what she finds so unthinkable. Difficulties for parents by no means come to an end when their daughter is admitted to hospital. When the young anorexic woman is admitted to a situation in which there is marked conflict between herself and her helpers, mothers are very often caught in the cross-fire. Typically, parents begin by agreeing with the doctors and nursing staff, trying to encourage the anorexic women to co-operate and hoping that it will become easier for her. Often, as time progresses, mothers in particular begin to sympathise more and more with their daughters. They, after all, are likely to understand fairly accurately how she feels about weight gain. This, in my experience, can cause profound difficulties within families. If the mother 'takes the daughter's side', then she is opposing attempts to help her; if she maintains her support for the medical authorities, she will not only cross swords with her daughter but will also experience herself as having abandoned her. This is always a very sad state of affairs. It quite often results in parents removing their daughters from hospital 'against medical advice'. It can also cause a great deal of conflict between mothers and other family members. In treatment situations where there is conflict between the anorexic woman and her helpers, parents can, in my experience, never remain neutral. They will inevitably be drawn into the conflict in one way or another. The only way to avoid conflict and the resulting unhappiness to families is to try to avoid treatment situations in which such difficulties are generated.

Parents, other family members and friends should always be

carefully informed about the treatment the anorexic woman is undergoing. They should be encouraged to discuss it with the staff and to question it, if they are not entirely in agreement. The more openness and free discussion which can be encouraged between the anorexic woman, her family and her helpers, the more likely is the outcome to be productive and positive.

The use of drugs

It is not at all uncommon for anorexic women who are hospitalised for weight gain to be prescribed psychotropic drugs.

The drugs most commonly used are those which have a tranquillising effect; they tend to keep the woman calm and relieve some of the anxiety which goes with the taking in of large amounts of food. In short, they lower her resistance to weight gain. Using the analysis suggested earlier, drugs tend to subdue the part of the woman which desperately wants to stay thin. They treat the aspects of her personality which the medical authorities define as sick. In *her* terms, drugs weaken the strong part of herself. They encourage her to be weak and sleepy and slothful. In my terms, drugs temporarily annihilate the very part of her which we might wish to have access to.

Clearly, the use of drugs might sometimes be regarded as a kindness. The woman who is severely undernourished has to eat in order to survive. Why not relieve some of her anxiety about doing so? Surely using drugs will only make it easier? While this is in one sense true, we have to bear in mind that drugs only have a temporary effect. In her lucid moments, between doses, the anorexic woman is painfully aware that she is being induced to do something which she very strongly disapproves of. If our ultimate aim is to help women to nourish themselves appropriately because they value themselves enough to do so, to begin the process by inducing an abnormal mental state may in the long run be counter-productive.

This is not to say that drugs might not sometimes be used as a life-saving measure; that is a very different matter. I do believe however that unless a woman is admitted to hospital as a real medical emergency (and in my experience, this is the exception rather than the rule), women who are in an anorexic state should be consulted about the use of drugs in their own particular case.

If you want to improve your nutritional condition, but feel that your own levels of anxiety are likely to be too high for you to manage this, you may well choose to use drugs to help you with the process. Some women however prefer to engage in the struggle in a state of clear consciousness. It may produce more anxiety, but at least they retain the feeling of being in control of what they are doing. Weight increase is an issue which is riven with conflict for the anorexic woman. Sooner or later, these conflicts will have to be faced and resolved; the use of drugs simply allows the woman to engage in the process of resolution later rather than sooner.

It used to be believed that insulin was a useful drug in the treatment of anorexia. I have personal knowledge of its use some four or five years ago. Anorexic women tell me that it is still sometimes used. The use of insulin is, to my mind, misguided in principle. The only effect of the drug on anorexic women (apart from occasionally sending them into a coma) is to increase appetite. Anorexia is not a disorder of appetite. The appetite becomes distorted after prolonged starvation, but recovered anorexics are well able to acknowledge that they were indeed hungry on many occasions during their anorexic phase. Anorexia is an attempt to deny appetite, to rise above appetite and everything which appetite implies. Increasing the needs of the body with appetite-inducing drugs merely serves to intensify the conflicts which the woman feels about satisfying the needs of her body. There is more chance that the woman will 'give in', will succumb to her hunger, but without a radical change in her attitude, her will to nourish herself remains unchanged.

I have heard of the use of anti-depressants and even of electro-convulsive therapy in the treatment of anorexia. This may be because the medical staff recognise that the anorexic woman is depressed. However, it seems likely that the depression is secondary to the anorexia; anorexics often become depressed when they begin to put on weight. This is not the kind of depression which will vanish with the use of drugs or other medical procedures. I can see no place at all for these kinds of treatments.

Anorexia seems to be the kind of problem which attracts fashionable treatments. A few years ago, zinc was put forward as a nutritional supplement which would 'cure' anorexia. This was presumably based on the assumption that anorexia is a physical illness brought about by nutritional deficiency. Of course it would be wonderful, miraculous even, if all the suffering of anorexics and their families could be cured by a pill. My experience, and that of dozens of recovered anorexics who have spoken to me, is that it is much more difficult than that. In the following chapter I try to say something about the complex process of change. But human nature being what it is, I am sure people will continue to search for short cuts and that others will be only too pleased to claim to supply them.

What should we say in summary about current trends in the treatment of anorexia? Without doubt, we can say that there is too much emphasis on the hospitalisation of women with an anorexic disorder. In terms of the resources available, there is great imbalance. Hospital treatment is readily available, whereas long-term counselling is very hard to find. Many women are sent into hospital who need not have to undergo such a painful experience, simply for the lack of available alternatives.

With the exception of a very few progressive units, hospital treatment has changed little in the last decade. Its effects are still potentially destructive and it can create as many difficulties as it solves.

There are and probably will continue to be some women with anorexia who remain untreated for so long that they actually need refeeding treatment. For them, hospital treatment, geared to their needs for nutritional first aid, is the right initial method of treatment.

If skilled counselling and psychotherapy were widely available, there is reason to believe that their numbers might be small.

6
Resolving the conflicts

Setting the scene

This chapter is addressed to, and designed to be of use to anyone who has reason to talk with a woman who is anorexic. I hope it will contribute to the understanding of those professional groups who most often find themselves involved: counsellors, social workers, psychologists, psychiatrists, general practitioners, nurses and teachers. But I hope too that it will be read by anorexic women themselves and by their families. They, as much as anyone else, need to learn about approaches to the treatment of their difficulties which are neither technical nor mystifying.

I have been at something of a loss as to what to call the kind of treatment I have in mind. To talk about 'counselling' implies a process which is rather straightforward and ordinary and which contains an element of advice-giving. The process I am thinking of is not at all like that. To write of 'psychotherapy' brings to mind psychoanalysis and the couch. 'Therapy', its diminutive form, has echoes of 'encounter' and the primitive outpouring of feelings. The process of discovery, of clarification and redefinition which seems so useful to anorexic women is neither mundane nor mysterious. It is in fact both simple and complex – but above all it is *clear*.

My decision therefore is to refer to the 'talking treatments' I want to describe as 'counselling', 'therapy' and 'psychotherapy' – interchangeably. If this decision does nothing else, it may convince professional helpers from a variety of disciplines that they should not exclude themselves from the possibility of working with anorexic women by virtue of what they call themselves.

Those of us who engage in work with anorexic clients have more serious problems to contend with than what we call ourselves. The first and most central of those problems is that we may not in the first instance have 'clients' at all. Women who have been treated for anorexia in a situation where the focus is on weight gain rather than therapy have learnt that treatment means being forced to do things and to give things up. Treatment is always associated with something unpleasant and with a struggle of wills. Anorexic women who have experienced this kind of treatment actually become very resistant to 'interference'. And it is often as interference that they interpret any attempt to engage them in talking about their difficulties.

Helpers are perceived as people who try to coerce. The anorexic woman has learnt how to deal with this; she resists, either by active rejection or by appearing to comply but secretly feeling that she knows best.

For these reasons, I think that the counsellor is likely to be more successful if she works outside the refeeding aspects of the treatment.[1]

In the previous chapter I suggested that nutritional treatments are often undertaken without sufficient thought as to whether they are really necessary or likely to be beneficial. Sometimes, a counsellor who is not involved with a residential institution such as a hospital might be a preferable alternative to try first. If we can avoid the unhelpful associations of treatment with coercion, then we will certainly be making the task of working on real problems very much easier. If the woman is already engaged in nutritional treatments, there are advantages in the counsellor or therapist keeping quite apart from that process. It the counsellor is also one of the feeders, she will automatically and correctly be seen as part of the coercive system within which, as we have seen, the anorexic symptoms flourish. It will also be more difficult for the woman to take a look in therapy at the effects of her refusal to eat on those around her, and at the meaning of her own insistence on being coerced.

Women in an anorexic phase find it initially very difficult to accept any kind of help with their difficulties; they have found a solution which in its own crippling way works for them and they are very unsure indeed about giving it up. Our aim, in the earliest stages of counselling, is to make it as easy as possible for the anorexic woman to say 'yes' to help. In my experience, it is much easier for her to accept therapeutic help from someone who is not involved in a refeeding struggle. Hilde Bruch disagrees on this point[2] and favours a more integrated approach. This may reflect her own clinical experience in a setting in which she works as a therapist, but has control of the weight restitution programme. If we are able to establish the counselling situation as distinct from the nutritional one, how then should counsellors deal with the issue of weight and possible weight restitution? Over time, I have developed a way of handling this issue which I find helpful. I often refer to it as a 'contract'.[3] In fact, it could more accurately be described as a delineation of responsibility. I, as a counsellor, am not willing, nor indeed able, to take responsibility for my client's nutritional well-being. No one can ensure that another adult human being eats adequate amounts of food. If my client wants to work with me at attempting to understand something about the real nature of her difficulties, then she must maintain at least a minimal level of nutritional health. If she feels at any point that she cannot continue to do this without help, then she must enlist some help. If the outcome is that she has to go into hospital in order to keep herself well enough to continue with therapy, then she must be prepared to do that too. I do not have any sanctions beyond the therapeutic situation itself. The only power I have is the possibility of stopping the therapy if she becomes drastically underweight and too ill to use it. In my experience this happens surprisingly rarely. The 'contract', or division of responsibilities is in itself a therapeutic pointer. What I am conveying is that her body is her own responsibility and no one else's. I do not own it or have jurisdiction over it, and it is not something we will fight over. Sometimes in families, children's bodies are considered to be the responsibility and terrain of their mothers. One of the fundamental anorexic assertions is that she and no one else can control this wayward thing. All too often, traditional treatments have challenged her rights and have asserted their control over her body. The response is predictable; she stamps her foot, both outwardly and inwardly, and erects her own barriers. In counselling we need to convey to women in an anorexic phase that there are good and right reasons for them to look after their bodies. This is not to do with satisfying other people's wishes and needs, but because the body is part of the woman and deserves nourishment just as much as her spirit does. It is her task to provide it with that nourishment and although it will not be easy for her, help is available should she need it.

This kind of agreement sets a therapeutic situation off on the right footing. It allows the client to maintain control of that area which is so precious to her, but it makes her truly responsible for doing so. It also indicates that therapy is a valuable thing; it is something which she may have to struggle hard to keep hold of. The therapist can sympathise with her efforts to maintain her weight but she cannot do it for her, nor can she force the client to do it. Such an agreement is also good for the counsellor. One of the most difficult aspects of the work with anorexic clients is the wish on the part of the therapist to solve the client's problems for her, to save her, ultimately, to eat for her. All these wishes, apart from being impossible, are dangerous. The purpose of counselling is to enable the woman to take care of herself. It is as well that we remind ourselves at the outset of the real limitation of our powers. While stressing that weight is the responsibility of the client, the counsellor must beware of setting up assumptions that the client will be able to gain weight just as and when it is necessary. Indeed, it is as well to make it clear that this is not an expectation.

As one woman remarked when referring to a previous experience in therapy, 'All he ever said to me was "eat, gain weight". That's like telling you to go away and solve the problem and come back when you have.'

Beginnings

If the focus of counselling is not to be on weight gain, how then do we proceed? How do we set about engaging the client in the shared process of unravelling the past and making the present a less confusing territory to inhabit?

The initial task is to enable the client to share her own perceptions of her life, however confused and unclear these may be. It is important to remember that this may be the woman's first opportunity to attempt such a thing. Traditionally, helpers have told anorexic women what to do.

In return, they expect to hear of her attempts to do what she is told. In hospital settings, no one is at all interested in the 'anorexic' aspects of the woman's experience – only in her attempts to overcome them.

There are several reasons why it is vital for her to be able to tell us in detail what her world is like. She needs to know that we realise how terribly difficult her life is. She can only know this if she herself has told us. She will not assume that we understand the constant torment which comes from her continual preoccupation with food. She will assume we do not understand how distorted all her relationships have become, how she feels compelled to deceive the people who care about her, how staying thin is, frighteningly, more important than any of them. She will assume we cannot understand all this because she expects she will also have such a distorted relationship with us. The fact that the counsellor is able to accept all this without shock or surprise, and to accept it in a spirit of sympathy, comes as quite a revelation. Counsellors need to be very good listeners. Women in general are very sensitive to our audience. We intuitively 'pick up' when we are not really being heard. Anorexic women are especially sensitive to other people's responses. They have lived their lives up to the point of the anorexic episode 'intuitively' knowing what other people expect, think and feel. In fact, of course, it is not at all difficult to listen with genuine interest and sympathy to what anorexic clients have to say. As soon that is, as the counsellor can abandon her need to challenge, criticise and prematurely change her client's anorexic life. If women were able to abandon the ravaging symptom of anorexia simply by being argued with, there would be no need for counsellors at all!

It is often said that anorexics all say the same things. This is true – but only for the first few minutes. The preoccupation with food and weight is universal, as is the terror of losing control, of eating and becoming horribly fat and bloated. But beyond that, if they can be encouraged to share a more detailed version of their worlds, one encounters a rich variety of feelings, perceptions and muddles.

One client's image of herself as the 'pre-raphaelite boy' would never have come to light if she had not been encouraged to talk in detail about her 'anorexicness'. Another client was able to describe her wish to be nothing more than a little dormouse which lay curled up all day being stroked by its mother, with no expectation from anyone that it should ever do anything else. The images of the pre-raphaelite boy and the dormouse proved to be useful landmarks in the process of recovery; both client and therapist knew exactly what was being given up.

The anorexic woman needs to be able to confront us with her ambivalence about treatment and recovery. As I described in the last chapter, she will sometimes enter the treatment situation full of hostility and determination that it will not touch her – not, at least, in the sense of changing her attitude to her own body. Sometimes women present themselves as passive and regretful that they are causing so much trouble. They are full of promises that they will not be 'difficult cases' for us and that they will really try to eat. Neither of these ways of presenting for therapy are helpful in themselves. Neither represents the whole picture. The sorry little anorexic full of good intentions is denying the side of her own experience which makes her cling to anorexia as though she will drown without it. The hostile, untouchable anorexic is denying the very thing which has brought her to therapy; the desperate wish to be rid of her compulsions and to be at peace. It is not possible to work with half a woman. In order for therapy to continue, the therapist must, in the earliest stages, enable the woman to share both aspects of her experience. The conflict between getting 'well' and staying 'ill' must be out in the open between the anorexic woman and her counsellor. At the beginning there is no way of resolving these conflicting wishes; they simply have to be acknowledged and allowed to coexist. Some anorexic women, as soon as they come for counselling, are quite ready and able to respond to the opportunity to talk and to be listened to. Others feel too confused and initially mistrustful to be able to talk about themselves without some help. With clients like this, the counsellor has to be prepared at first to do most of the work. She has to be able to acknowledge that 'talking about it' is indeed difficult. Sometimes women who come for help believe that what we want is a complete account of their medical history. In fact what we really want is to get to understand them as people. But a woman who has been in an anorexic state for a long time may well have lost all sense of herself as a person. All of her feelings may have become submerged under her preoccupation with food and its avoidance. When this is the case, we need to work hard in order to enable her to return to thinking of herself and taking herself seriously as something other than a thin body. I sometimes find it helpful to share with her something of what I understand as the true nature of the anorexic plight.[4] I might say that I often find young women like her have a very low opinion of themselves, that they really don't have much confidence in themselves and don't like themselves very much. If she looks depressed or unhappy I might pick up on this and ask her if my hunch that she is unhappy is right. Can she tell me how she feels?

The reason for giving these leads is *not* to make her believe that I know exactly how she feels, but rather to help her to engage in the process of identifying her own feelings so that she can tell me.

The key to this approach is gentleness and patience. Anything harsh or assertive or 'clever' on the part of the therapist will frighten her. Everything which she has to contribute is valuable. If she says she does not know how she feels, this is not an occasion for the counsellor to look disappointed. Rather, she should express her interest in this 'not knowing'. It must, after all, make life very confusing and difficult if you do not know how you feel.

This sort of initial approach usually works and by the end of the first session we can establish a common goal and interest – that of understanding together more about her.

Unravelling the issues – ongoing therapy

The process of recovery from an anorexic phase can be summed up as the process of the woman finding herself. The counsellor's task can then be seen as one of assisting in that discovery. It is not for the counsellor to find the woman – a mistake which workers can make – but rather for the woman to come to see herself.

This understanding carries implications for the ways in which therapists can work effectively with anorexic women. Some models of therapy, those based on psychoanalysis in particular, rely upon the wisdom and theoretical knowledge of the therapist, shared with the client to produce change. The therapist's job is to listen to the client and then to work on the material which she produces, to interpret it and offer it back in a changed form. This kind of technique works very well with some sorts of clients. It is not, however, a very useful way of working with anorexic clients, not, at least, until very late on in therapy when much of the ground work has been covered.

Anorexic women feel powerless and ineffective. By telling them what their lives *really* mean, we are encouraging them to persist in the belief that they are incompetent.

An example. Ruth came for her session saying that she had been upset by a girl at college who she felt had cut her out of a conversation and ignored her. 'I don't understand why she hates me so much,' were her first words on the subject. Ruth is a brilliant and beautiful girl who has grown up with the sense of having no natural talent or good looks, but always having to struggle to keep one step ahead of the rest. If she relaxed for a moment, she felt, she would fall to the bottom of the class and be rejected by everyone. Her deep-seated insecurities about herself and her own worth led her to take a defensive and somewhat flippant attitude to the world. She would adopt a posture of superiority and dismissiveness towards other people and never reveal to them her need to be cared for and appreciated by them.

If, however, the therapist had attempted at this stage to explain the incident to Ruth in terms of her own defensiveness, Ruth would not only have concluded, 'So that's why my friend hates me so much'; she would also have had no option but to defend herself against the therapist's explanation by denying it. Instead she was invited to look with the therapist at the incident in more detail. To describe what had happened, to think about her own feelings at the time and to consider her own responses. She had obviously found it impossible to welcome the other girl into the conversation with an encouraging smile. Why was it so hard for her? Ruth found the process of reconstructing the situation difficult and upsetting. She needed the therapist's understanding and support to be able to manage it. Finally she blurted out, 'But I'm afraid to be nice to people. Suppose they still don't like me?' From this point, Ruth was able to make slow but certain progress in changing and adapting her ways of relating to people. As she unfroze a little and began to reveal something of her own needs, she enjoyed more positive feedback and began to experience herself as likeable.

A great deal of work with anorexic women is of this detailed and painstaking kind. Both therapist and client need a lot of patience. But in reality, there are no short cuts. The therapist's attempts to tell the client about herself, to explain her own behaviour to her, will be felt to be invasive and wounding. They will therefore have to be rejected. This rejection can either be of an overt kind – the therapist's version of events is denied – or the client can passively agree, offer a polite consent which leaves the counsellor knowing that her wisdom has not penetrated the surface.

It is very important for counsellors to understand that their interpretations are rejected because they are *wounding*. If anorexia is an attempt to assert autonomy, to cover up a lack of self-identity, and at the same time to find one, then to be told yet again who you are and what you could or should be, is bound to be unhelpful. Anorexia also represents a kind of attempt at self-sufficiency. It is an assertion that no one is needed and that no one will be allowed in. If the counsellor attempts to storm the portals, she will be repulsed.[5]

In Miranda's case, I was particularly surprised by the way in which even my most gentle and respectful reflections seemed to wound and anger her. If she described a situation in which she had clearly been unhappy and ill at ease, my attempts to focus on or even to sympathise with her discomfort would result in a polite but firm denial that this was what she had been feeling. One day in a session, Miranda was describing some time she had recently spent with her mother. She described the way in which she had very properly and skilfully excused herself from spending further time with a friend of her mother's whom she found tedious. Afterwards, she had said to her mother, 'I hope you didn't think I was being unsociable.' Her mother's reply was, 'It's all right. I know you find it difficult in social situations.' Miranda's initial comment to me was that her mother was very understanding. On further investigation, it became clear that mother's interpretation of Miranda's behaviour had been quite wrong. She did not have difficulty in social situations. On the contrary, social charm was not by any means a deficiency of Miranda's. Far from being understanding, Miranda's mother had misunderstood. Miranda had not been in difficulty, she had been bored! The interesting point was that Miranda had not even challenged her mother's explanation of her behaviour in her own mind. Mother was certain to be right. The continuing experience of being mis-explained without any conscious awareness that it was happening had made it almost impossible for her to accept any help from me in working towards her own definition of herself. All too often when we offer anorexic women explanations of themselves, we simply repeat and reopen an earlier wound.

Following our careful reinterpretation of Miranda's conversation with her mother and of many similar conversations, she became able to deal more effectively not only with her mother, but with me too! She became less fearful that by trying to understand her, I would in fact misur.Jerstand and destroy her.

The task of therapy or counselling is, more than anything else, the task of translating the symptoms of anorexia into the realities and details of everyday life. The woman who is struggling and fighting to keep control of her size and shape, to keep herself in charge of her eating lest it take her over, is at another level, desperately trying to assert some kind of control on her own life. The woman who is afraid of her need and longing for food and for the good and comforting things in life is, in a different way, afraid that her own feelings, needs and longings will be too much for herself and for other people to bear. Her need to be The Thinnest, to achieve the perfect body where other women fail, points to a more broad-based search for perfection which is driven by self-doubt. She cannot evaluate her own achievements any more realistically than she can judge her size. She lives with the fear of being discovered to be incompetent. The difficulty of working with such women lies in the very severity of the symptoms. She cannot be aware of the real issues which lie behind her obsessions with food and weight because the feelings which these evoke are so strong that they obscure everything else.

In my experience, working with such problems in the abstract is of no help at all. We may elicit agreement from the woman that these are her 'real' difficulties, but unless we can work with her on those areas of *her* life where they are really evident, the work will have little meaning. This means that we have to listen and wait. Sometimes the issues on which we need to work are presented in a very hidden and opaque way.

Alison appeared to me a most mature and competent young woman for her seventeen years. Her difficulties with food had been going on for about a year and a half although in the few months before she came for counselling they had become much worse and she had lost a good deal of weight in a short time. She began to make herself sick regularly after eating and guiltily confessed that at times she became very depressed. She was at a loss to know why this had all happened. Her family she described as very 'supportive'. She felt herself to be the favourite, particularly of her father, though he was always careful not to give her more attention than her two brothers. She had done very well with her O-levels and although not considered brilliant, everyone, including herself, believed that if she continued to work hard, she would gain entry into a college of higher education without difficulty. She was going to be a primary school teacher, she told me. History and geography were her best subjects, but she believed she would be best suited teaching a range of subjects to younger children. Did she have experience of working with young children, I asked? Yes, she worked at a playgroup in the neighbourhood in her school holidays and on occasion had helped out at the local infants school. On the face of it, she sounded to be a very thoughtful and sensible young person, who had her life well planned! It was when I asked her what it was she liked about working with small children that she began to become confused. I said that I sometimes found little ones a bit boring. Alison looked puzzled. It was not a question of *what* she liked about the work; she had never even thought about whether she liked it at all. We talked about friends. Why did she choose to be friends with some girls rather than others? Again, the puzzled look. Alison did not choose friends; she waited to be chosen. What did she especially enjoy about geography and history? In truth, she never really thought about that either. She had been told she was good at them, so she *did* them.

Here was a young woman whose life really was out of control. It was all going well, but she was not at the helm. Everything was well planned, but by whom? The only aspect of life which she could really control was her size and shape. Her thinness was her own achievement. She fought hard for it and could not give it up until she had made some progress in other areas of her life. As things turned out, she gave up her A-level course, spent a year or so in a series of temporary jobs, and finally settled for a career in nursing. The last time I heard from her, she was working as a staff nurse, but was just about to go into temporary 'retirement' to have her first baby.

A success story perhaps. But it was not as simple as I have made it sound. In the process of defining and discovering her own identity, Alison became a much more assertive and 'difficult' young woman. Her family were most concerned and genuinely wanted to understand what was happening to her. But they were horrified at the idea of her giving up school and abandoning her planned career. They themselves needed a lot of help with this situation. Finally, after a great deal of distress, Alison's mother decided, 'I don't really understand all this, but if Alison needs time to sort things out for herself, she'll have it. I never did.'

It sounds easy. But for a family who did not normally allow themselves the freedom to make mistakes, it really was not.

Sometimes, the anorexic symptoms themselves, or the consequences of them, come to play a very important role in the woman's life. 'Being anorexic' might, for example, provide a good reason for not going to parties or other social gatherings. In this instance, we need to help the woman to evaluate whether or not she *wants* to go to parties at the moment. In a surprising number of cases I have found that she does not. Parties were always experienced as stressful and difficult situations. 'Getting better' then implies a return to these social predicaments which she feels better off without. Until she can learn to say 'no' to unwelcome invitations, she will need a symptom which says 'no' for her. This is part of the process of taking control of life.

I have found the role of the symptom to be particularly striking in the lives of bulimic women. It is a symptom which can be very time consuming. Some women spend several hours of each day buying and eating food. The cycle continues through the self-induced vomiting and is completed by the ritual cleaning of the bathroom and disposal of any remaining food. It usually ends with the woman falling asleep exhausted. The important question to ask here is what would she do with her evening if she did not do this? The answer of course is that the symptom prevents her from confronting what to do with free or unstructured time. Until she is able to look this problem squarely in the face, to confront her own feelings of isolation and alienation when she is alone, giving up the symptom will be very difficult. Using unstructured time is, I think, a problem for most women who suffer from disorders of eating. I suspect that in fact it may be a problem which very many women experience. As women, we are not generally taught to own our time. Traditionally, a woman's time, even her leisure time, is punctuated by meeting the needs of other people. Getting to the shops before they close, picking the children up from school and of course, getting the meal on the table 'on time'. When they step outside these traditional roles, many women experience real fear at the prospect of unpunctuated time. A preoccupation with food certainly helps to fill the gaps and provide focal points in the day. The bulimic woman may deal with her difficulties about time by spending a great deal of it absorbed in her rituals about eating itself, with the inevitable cleansing process which follows. The anorexic woman who is abstaining from food will still occupy herself to a large extent by thinking about food, planning what to eat and what not to eat, reading calorie charts (and sometimes recipe books too!).

Another interesting and important aspect of the disorder, especially for bulimic women, is the secrecy which it entails. Quite often women who habitually make themselves sick keep the problem a secret from the person or people they live with. Here we have to consider the possibility that the woman really does need to have secrets. Does she find the people around her to be intrusive? What else does she have in her life which she does not share with anyone? Before she can give up the symptom, she may need to develop some other 'secret' aspect of her life which is less self-destructive. She needs to learn that it is perfectly all right to have parts of herself which she does not share with anyone. Surprisingly, a number of women I have worked with feel that to need to have psychological space and privacy is in itself abnormal. Particularly women who are in a long-term relationship or married tend to think that the need to have a secret aspect of themselves which they do not share with their partners, must indicate that there is something wrong with the relationship. The anorexic or bulimic symptom gives them a reason for doing just this, but in the guise of an 'illness'.

Escaping from unwelcome situations, using the symptom to say 'no', structuring time and finding privacy are only some possible roles that women's symptoms can play in our lives. Not all women will use symptoms in these particular ways. It is however, vitally important to consider what the symptom is doing before it can be given up.

Recovery

What does recovery from an anorexic episode consist in, and how is it achieved? How does the process I have described lead to a 'recovery'?

To answer the first question, of what constitutes recovery, we have to do away with the idea that weight is a reliable indicator of progress. Of course it is necessary for a woman to achieve a reasonable and steady weight which is consistent with her height and body shape before she can properly be said to have recovered. The weight at which she finally settles may or may not be the same as the weight she had before the anorexic episode. She may end up a bit bigger or a bit smaller. It really does not matter at all. There is no such thing as an ideal weight and anything which is consistent with health is appropriate. The aspect of recovery which has to do with weight might more properly be described as a giving up of the compulsion to maintain weight at an artificially low level. The interesting and important point about weight restoration is that in my experience, it may be one of the last aspects of recovery to be achieved, not one of the first. Just as the origins of anorexia do not lie in weight loss, so recovery from the disorder does not reside in its gain.

The recovered anorexic is someone who has a sense of being in charge of her own life. She is able to make decisions about herself, based on her real perceptions of what she does and does not want. She has self-respect and an accurate sense of her own worth. She is not someone who does not have any problems. Life is difficult. No one can or should live in such a way as to avoid these difficulties. A woman who has recovered from an anorexic phase is prepared to take them on for what they are and not simply to take refuge in the pursuit of a physical and spiritual ideal.

How can counselling or therapy help to bring about such change? This is a difficult question to answer, because the process of recovery is different for everyone. I must confess too, that recovery often takes me by surprise. It has often happened that when I am feeling particularly 'stuck' with a client she suddenly appears to make a breakthrough which takes us into the home straight. Of course, the change is not really sudden. It is simply that my focus has been too narrow. I have been feeling that her eating pattern is as stuck as ever and this has made it difficult for me to see that her relationships with colleagues at work have changed and blossomed in new and exciting ways or that her relationship with her mother is now no longer the central focus of our work. The final step of letting go of the anorexic symptom will follow this hard work, not precede it.

When I first experienced surprise at someone's seemingly sudden recovery, I looked back over the work and decided that I must simply have been unobservant. But gradually I began to see that this element of surprise was the rule rather than the exception. I think there are a number of ways in which we can account for this. As the woman begins to focus her and my attention on the real difficulties in life, much of her former certainty about what she is doing leaves her. She becomes more confused, if anything more desperate in her desire to keep control of her body; she is after all beginning to take some risks with herself out in the real world. It is easy to mistake this desperation for regression rather than to see it as progress. I believe also that the final step of changing her way of eating is something which she must control. If she abandons her symptoms to reassure me rather than because she feels able to live without them, then it would be a suspect kind of recovery. The therapist is taught once again that it is *her* life and things will happen in *her* time.

The giving up of the symptom, or rather the beginnings of an attempt to give it up, is not by any means the end of the story. We must remember that the recovering anorexic has been living in a world of hunger and self-denial, possibly for a very long time. I have never known a recovered anorexic who did not go through a period of chaos around food during the process of recovery. Sometimes this is a fairly short and contained period during which she tries out different ways of eating and finally establishes some guidelines for herself. Sometimes it is a more prolonged and traumatic experience, in which she feels as though she has abandoned one, very safe symptom for a series of much more dangerous ones. The counsellor must be prepared for this and be able to see it for what it is. The client will panic and feel that all her worst fears about loss of control have come true. It is important that the worker does not do the same. Our main task at this stage is to ensure that the new difficulties about food do not become an entrenched pattern. We have continually to look forward, to point to her successes with managing food, to help her to analyse how she managed to eat exactly what she wanted on one occasion, but much more than she wanted on another. This is a new and frightening stage in her development. She needs help to approach it in a spirit of discovery, as a relearning process. In fact the counsellor needs to work with the new phase in exactly the same way as she has worked all along. She will sympathise when things go wrong, but she will want to look in detail at actual situations so that they can be properly understood and learned from. This can often be one of the most difficult aspects of recovery for anorexic women. That is why it is so cruel to pronounce her 'cured' after a hospital programme of weight restitution: if she is left to founder alone with her new-found 'freedom' in the area of eating, she may very well end up with problems just as severe as she had before. After a period of counselling or therapy, we at least know that she has the basic equipment and orientation for handling these new difficulties. She has, after all, chosen the time to try.

When should counselling end?

This is another difficult question. We have to remember that we are not there to help the woman solve her problems for the rest of her life. Our job is to enable her to take that on for herself. My own experience is that therapy with anorexics should probably end when they have difficulty in finding space for appointments in their diaries! In fact, a gradual phasing out is usually more appropriate than a complete break. A woman may need for a long while to know that we are 'there' and available if *she* should decide she needs some help. But particularly in the case of very young people, I do not favour continuing therapy for longer than is really necessary. We do young clients no service by encouraging them to think of therapy as a way of life. There are (or should be) much more interesting directions to look than inwards.

Most anorexic women will need to work at their difficulties for at least a year, some for much longer – perhaps up to four years. So it is important for counsellors when they begin to work with anorexic women to acknowledge that they are making a long-term commitment.

Prognosis: the outcomes of treatment

Opinions vary widely as to how many women recover from anorexic episodes and how many do not. The difficulty in arriving at a comprehensive view lies in the fact that we can never be sure we are comparing like with like. What one doctor counts as 'recovery' may not satisfy the criteria of another. We can never be certain that the women who are being compared had equally serious difficulties in the first place. And we also have no idea how many women recover spontaneously or with support from their friends and family and so never become part of the statistics. Or how many women *would* recover if offered a more sustained and sympathetic kind of help. These are all impossible questions to answer but we need to keep in mind this lack of information.

The evidence which we have can seem somewhat bleak and depressing – we hear so much about the women who fail to recover. And yet most readers are probably acquainted with several women who have successfully recovered from anorexia – but who have never felt the need to mention the fact! If we had access to the complete picture of what happens to women following an anorexic episode, there is no doubt that we should feel more optimistic.

With this in mind, let us turn now to the variety of possible outcomes.

Death is a comparatively rare outcome, though it is probably only as rare as it is because most anorexic women have people in their lives who take active steps to prevent it from occurring. In an acute anorexic episode, some, though certainly not all, women would starve themselves to death if not prevented from doing so. This is not because they really want to die. It is because they simply do not believe they will.

But even bearing that in mind, I believe that death from suicide is more of a risk than death from the physical consequences of the disorder. The time when many women with anorexia have suicidal feelings is the period following enforced weight gain, when they are appalled at the new 'fat' shape they have taken on, feel utterly at a loss as to how to live with it and in addition may find their eating chaotic and uncontrollable. This is certainly a time of great vulnerability. The unsupported anorexic will try to deal with it by again losing weight (which is why traditional treatment methods have such a high readmission rate). If she cannot get her eating 'under control' and begin to lose weight again, she will feel depressed and desperate enough to make suicide a real possibility.

A second possible outcome, and one which is very much more common, is that the woman makes a partial recovery. That is to say she gains enough weight to keep her alive, but then maintains it at an artificially low level, sometimes for many years. Although on the whole she manages to keep out of hospital, her life continues to be utterly dominated by the desire to avoid food. She may manage to go to work, but has little time or energy or inclination for any sort of social life. Her life becomes increasingly narrow and inward looking. This is in fact a form of chronic anorexia. It is often brought about by a humiliating and unhelpful experience in hospital. All that the woman learns from it is that she will do anything to avoid going back. This group of women are particularly difficult, though not impossible, to work with in counselling.

Another highly undesirable outcome is that of the woman whose 'anorexic will' has been broken by too harsh an experience of hospitalisation and who learns to control her weight by making herself sick. This at first appears to her to be the magic solution. In fact she is merely replacing one set of symptoms with another and is no nearer at all to discovering where her real difficulties lie.

The whole picture, however, is not as depressing as it sounds. Almost all specialists in the field report that the majority of anorexics do recover.[6] One of the worrying features of their reports is that of those who recover sufficiently to be able to live creative and independent lives, a sizable proportion still retain some elements of their anorexic thinking and are often still quite preoccupied with food and weight. Sheila MacLeod[7] describes her own situation in this way in *The Art of Starvation*. At the time when she wrote the book, although 'recovered' in most senses of the word, her weight was still a source of anxiety to her and it seems that she felt in some way vulnerable to another 'bout' of anorexia when life became particularly difficult. It is because of experiences like Sheila's that it is sometimes said that no one truly recovers from anorexia, that once anorexic a woman will always have difficulties and preoccupations in the area of food and she will always be vulnerable to relapse into an anorexic state.

I am delighted to be able to say that this simply is not true. It is my experience that where a resolution of the difficulties that led to an anorexic experience does take place, the woman is no longer vulnerable to further anorexic episodes and is no more neurotic about food than anyone else!

The reasons for this are not difficult to see. Anorexia is a symptom which can only flourish in the woman who lacks self-confidence and who has not found a way of being in the world which is both comfortable and realistic. She is a woman who cannot ask for the help and support she needs, but who experiences herself as incompetent if she cannot, alone, achieve perfection. The recovered anorexic on the other hand is able to feel at home in the world, to evaluate herself realistically and let go of her need to be lonely and perfect. Interestingly, recovered anorexics are rather wonderful people. This is not an experience which leaves women untouched. For many, the overcoming of it is a real point of growth. This is not to say that they will never have any difficulties in life again. But I think it is to say that they will not attempt to solve them in this particularly sterile and self-destructive way.

7
Recognition and Action

Throughout this book, I have been careful to try to avoid giving direct advice. I am convinced that when you are caught up in an acutely anorexic episode, the very last thing you need is to be told what to do, what to think or how you ought to understand things. I am, however, frequently asked for advice, often over the telephone, by people I do not have the chance to get to know personally. To say, 'I don't give advice' is not good enough on those occasions and at this stage in the book, I feel it is not good enough either.

I will therefore attempt to say something which might be useful to those of you who think you might be suffering from anorexia. My comments will necessarily be very general, because I do not know *you*. And do bear in mind that in your particular case, I might possibly be wrong!

If you are, or think you may be, suffering from anorexia, it is vitally important that you obtain some help while the problem is still in its early stages. It is very much easier to work with at this time, and the chances of a successful recovery are very much greater and likely to be achieved in a relatively short period of time.

You cannot rely on your parents or your teachers or your friends to recognise that you have difficulties. Perhaps they have already recognised a problem, but unless you yourself can see that you are in trouble, there is very little that they can do. The important point about early detection and recognition of anorexia is that *you* need to discover that you need some help.

Often, the problem will not be that you do not know you have difficulties, but that you are afraid to ask for help.

Anorexia is, as we have seen, an attempt at self-sufficiency. It is a denial of any weakness and of all needs. You therefore have a built-in problem. For you to admit that you are not really coping with life very well is to do the very thing which the anorexic symptom is designed to avoid. You may feel very bad and unhappy, but you may desperately want to hold on to your symptom as well. Staying thin, and maybe getting just a little bit thinner, may seem to be the only thing worth living for. Sometimes too, you may have heard stories about being sent to hospital, kept in bed and fattened up. Well-meaning friends may have threatened you with this prospect in order to try to scare you into eating more. The temptation is always to resist asking for help *yet*. To struggle on for a bit longer in the hope that something will change.

But if you think you might be anorexic, the only important thing is for you to recognise it as *soon* as you can bring yourself to do so. To encourage you to think carefully, and to make it more difficult for you to dismiss the idea, I will list some of the signs you might look for in yourself, and some of the questions you might ask yourself.

First of all, how much weight have you really lost? What is the heaviest you have ever been? What do you weigh now? I know these questions sound 'pushy', but you might be tempted to minimise your weight loss and you really do need to know the truth.

When other people express surprise or concern about your weight loss, how do you feel and react? Are you able to listen to them and think about it? Or does their concern make you feel defensive and 'got at'? If it is hard for you to face up to what is happening to your body, this may indicate that you are in some trouble. Perhaps part of you feels you should not really be trying to lose more weight, but another part does not want to stop doing it?

Have your periods stopped? This is an important diagnostic feature of anorexia. There is some doubt about why it actually happens, but often periods are affected quite early on, before very much weight has been lost. Of course, a variety of factors, physical and psychological can affect our menstrual cycles, but the loss of periods together with weight loss should make you suspect that anorexia might be the cause.

What about your attitude to food? Do you spend a lot of time thinking about it? What do you have in your life at the moment which is more important to you than avoiding food and controlling your weight?

If food seems like an enemy, if you can only see it as something which will be bad for you, make you fat and rob you of your sense of control, then you are certainly unhappy and probably in some sense anorexic.

How do you feel after you have eaten? Do you have a strong emotional reaction? What are the feelings? Guilt? Panic? A sense of failure? Feelings such as these should make you doubt that all is well.

If you can identify with some or all of these features of anorexia and believe that you have difficulties in this direction, think carefully now about whether you can afford to let the process just go on. It will not go away on its own. Remember that the sooner you begin to work at your difficulties, the easier it will be.

Try not to tell yourself that you have just been stupid, and that you really will eat more sensibly tomorrow. You are not stupid, and you cannot change yourself merely by an act of will.

Try not to think of anorexia as a personal failing. Surely it was actually an attempt to deal with your own feelings and to make yourself feel better?

Try to find someone you trust whom you can talk to. Someone who will listen to you. It might be a doctor, a college counsellor, an older friend, or another woman who has experienced anorexia. It is by sharing, by participating in relationships, not by trying to struggle on alone that life will eventually come to feel better.

Finding help

There is a great deal of treatment available for anorexic women at present. Most of it, unfortunately, is organised around the central locus of the hospital. This can mean that you will either be expected to become an in-patient in the hospital or to attend an out-patient clinic for appointments. As discussed earlier, in-patient treatment is unlikely to be appropriate for women who recognise early that they have difficulties. You may also feel quite resistent to accepting psychiatric out-patient appointments. So finding the sort of treatment which actually suits you may require some research.

You might want to begin by talking the problem over with your family doctor, or you might, in the first instance, prefer to contact one of the voluntary organisations listed at the end of this book.

Finding a counsellor can be difficult. You may have to shop around and be fairly persistent. If you want to try an out-patient counselling approach, tell your doctor what you want. Some psychiatrists offer very good out-patient therapy facilities, while others are less skilled in this kind of work. Some branches of Relate (formerly the Marriage Guidance Council) are prepared to work with anorexic women. Find out what your local branch has to say.

Be selective. Ask for what you want.

Similarly, if in-patient treatment is advised, or if you think you are unlikely to be able to maintain your weight without this kind of help, find out exactly what kind of service particular hospitals offer. Does the hospital have much experience of your kind of difficulty? Does it have a special unit for people with eating disorders? What kind of follow-up support can you expect when you leave hospital? How much say will you have about what happens to you? Go for a consultation, but do not feel obliged to accept whatever is offered. The voluntary organisations listed below may be able to put you in touch with someone who has experience of the hospital you have in mind.

It is only when women with eating disorders begin to assert what kind of treatment it is that they want, that we can expect existing facilities to change to meet their needs.

Self help

By 'self help' I do not mean continuing to struggle on trying to solve your problems on your own. Rather, I am thinking of the possibility of working together with other women, in a group, where problems which you have in common can be shared and worked on. There is no doubt that this can be a very valuable approach for some women. In particular, women who over-eat and make themselves sick often find enormous relief by working with other women who do the same.

In my experience, women who are in the middle of an acute anorexic episode often have difficulties working in groups. It can sometimes add to the stress in their lives, rather than relieving it.

A self-help approach is probably most useful for women either in the very earliest stages of an anorexic disorder, who have not become too withdrawn to be able to work at their difficulties, or for women who are well on the way to recovery but still need help and support to continue in the right direction.

Although useful, for many women, self help will probably not be enough. It can however be an important additional means of help, used in conjunction with, for example, individual counselling.

To mothers and other relatives, teachers, friends

If you think someone in your family or your social group might be suffering from anorexia, you probably feel at a loss as to what to do. The best way for you to assess whether or not your fears are based on something real is to think about what you know of her attitude to food and weight in general. A lot of women go on diets and some lose weight. They are certainly not all anorexic. Weight loss in itself can mean a number of different things. The woman might be suffering from some physical illness. She might be depressed and have genuinely lost her appetite. Remember that anorexia often begins with an accidental weight loss, due to illness or unhappiness. It will only turn into anorexia nervosa if the woman gets 'hooked' on losing weight and begins to use that as a way of solving other problems in life.

How do you know whether or not you are justified in being worried about this young woman? The 'normal dieter' will be able to talk about the sense of deprivation she feels at not being able to eat what she wants. She may show an obsessive interest in food, but on the whole she will be open about it. She will also proudly be able to tell you exactly how many pounds she has lost. The anorexic woman on the other hand will be vague and evasive about her weight loss. She will tend to underestimate it. She will deny that she is hungry or that she would like to eat the foods she resists. Her interest in food will be hidden, indirect. She may show much more interest in what you are eating than in her own meagre allowance.

Anorexic women, as distinct from women who lose weight for other reasons, also tend to adopt rather austere and self-punishing styles of life. They are likely to go in for what seem like excessive amounts of exercise by most people's standards. They are not much inclined to have fun and tend to approach life in a very serious sort of way. You might notice that your friend or relative has changed in this respect, that she no longer has the same capacity for enjoyment that she had before. You might notice too that she rejects comfort wherever she can. She will turn down the offer of a lift, saying she prefers to walk. She will sometimes wear insufficient clothes when the weather is cold, insisting that she does not feel it. She may become less open, more withdrawn, perhaps spending long periods of time alone. Friends as well as family tend to irritate her and she finds social interaction stressful.

. If, after considering all this, you feel you have reason to be concerned about her, say so.

How should you react?

I am so often asked this question by worried mothers that I feel I must make some attempt to answer it although I do not believe there are any rules, nor that there is really any way of doing the right thing.

The first and most important thing I can say is that you should give up any belief that you can cure her.

Parents, teachers and friends can sometimes be very *helpful* in the process of recovery, but family members in particular are usually quite the wrong people to undertake the task alone. The very fact of your close involvement will mean that your anxiety about the anorexic woman will be very high. This kind of personal anxiety makes it impossible for you to take on the counselling role with the woman concerned. You *can* be helpful, but don't expect too much of yourself.

Next, you need to try to understand her situation from her point of view, without of course needing to agree with it. This understanding on your part is important because it will mean that you are more likely to respond in an intuitive way to her immediate needs.

Try to remember that she is not doing all this on purpose to upset you. It will sometimes feel to you as though she is.

Try not to nag about food. It simply does not work. On the other hand, if you totally hide your feelings of concern about her physical condition, you will create a situation which is quite artificial.

The most important way in which you can help is by trying to help her to build up her self-confidence. At the same time you will need to help her to give up some of her perfectionism. She needs to know that she is quite good enough as she is.

Try to avoid comments like, 'You used to be such a pretty girl, and look at you now.' Or 'Have you any idea how much damage you are doing to your health?' She has enough on her mind already.

Don't keep asking her why she is doing all this – even in the most sympathetic way. She doesn't understand it any better than you do.

And don't worry all the time about saying the wrong thing. You would be super-human if you didn't. If you do happen to say or do something which you think has been hurtful, say so. Tell her that you find it difficult sometimes to respond helpfully. Then forget about it. Don't go away feeling guilty. You really haven't done anything terrible.

Finally, a word about taking care of yourself. I know how very, very worried mothers with anorexic daughters can sometimes become and how much you want to make everything right for your daughter. I have met many mothers in your position who have become depressed and indeed physically ill with the responsibility of it all. You really do have to try to look after yourself, and you do *not* have to be responsible for everyone else, even though that may not come easily to you. Make a conscious attempt to find some support for yourself, either from another family member, a friend or a counsellor. Remember that Anorexic Aid will be concerned about you as well as your daughter – and that you deserve as much help as you can find.

Some useful books

Here are some books which you might find helpful. For the reader with a more specialist interest, a fuller bibliography is provided.

Bruch, Hilde, *Eating Disorders: Obesity, Anorexia Nervosa and the Person Within*, Routledge and Kegan Paul, London, 1974. This is a rather big book, but good to dip into. Although a little dated now, it is written with such wisdom and sensitivity that it is well worth looking at.

Bruch, Hilde, *The Golden Cage*, Open Books, London, 1978. A delightful and very moving book. Short, clear and full of understanding.

Crisp, A.H., *Anorexia Nervosa: Let Me Be*, Academic Press, London, 1980. A scholarly, yet readable book, obviously based upon many years of experience.

Dana, M. and Lawrence, M., *Women's Secret Disorder: A New Understanding of Bulimia*, Grafton, London, 1988. My attempt, with Mira Dana, to understand something of the bulimic woman's experience.

Lawrence, M., editor, *Fed Up and Hungry: Women, Oppression and Food*, The Women's Press, London, 1987. A collection of papers on eating disorders by feminist academics and therapists.

MacLeod, Sheila, *The Art of Starvation*, Virago, London, 1981. A remarkable account of anorexia. Based on the author's own experience of the problem, it is a thorough review of the different approaches.

Moorey, J., *Living with Anorexia and Bulimia*, Manchester University Press, Manchester, 1991. A sensible and compassionate book, with a particularly good section on the family.

Palmer, R.L., *Anorexia Nervosa*, Penguin, London, 1980. A brief and clear account of the subject. A very useful introduction.

Shute, Jenefer, *Life-Size*, Secker and Warburg, London, 1992. A novel about anorexia.

8

The Anorexic Experience: A Story

by Will Pennycook

Never shall a young man,
Thrown into despair
By those great honey-coloured
Ramparts at your ear,
Love you for yourself alone
And not your yellow hair.

But I can get a hair-dye
And set such colour there,
Brown, or black, or carrot,
That young men in despair
May love me for myself alone
And not my yellow hair.

I heard an old religious man
But yesternight declare
That he had found a text to prove
That only God, my dear,
Could love you for yourself alone
And not your yellow hair.

W.B. YEATS

I lived with my sister, my mother and father and my grandmother, in a northern town. I was the baby; eight years younger than my sister. I was lively and cheerful; I think of it now, longingly, as my time of

118

exuberance and freedom. Old photographs provide me with a sense of my past; show me as I felt myself to be. The ones I love most are the ones taken with my father, when the family was on holiday by the sea. There I was, aged two or three, ready to run, and being held, securely, by my smiling father. The look on my face was one of excitement, high spirits and mischief. Others taken at the same time show different variations on the same theme: playing in the sand, falling in the water, running and jumping and singing. The old photographs bring with them all the attendant memories. That fervent curiosity, 'You're always saying "Why?" ': that hunger for knowledge about the world and how it worked (especially how it worked) and the ease with which that knowledge could be gained. One of my chief activities at that time was making up plays and stories. They have become part of the family folklore. I would boss and bully all my relations into sitting down, facing the window of the small living room and then, disappear behind the curtains only to reappear, with a fanfare of my own making, seconds later. Everyone would have to approve and applaud. When they talk about these activities, as they still do, I experience a mixture of cringing embarrassment and fierce pride. The little girl who created plays was not plagued by self-doubt or shyness; she was confident and proud. Of course, I was encouraged. My father and my aunts and uncles loved to tease me and they enjoyed my spirit. My mother, I suspect, felt embarrassed. Although I don't know.

My father enjoyed playing with me: at home he would tickle and play rough and tumble games. On holiday, we would play in the sea together. However, he always used to say, just when I was really beginning to enjoy myself, that he had had enough, 'Enough is as good as a feast.' He would then go back to my mother and my sister on the beach. I could never have enough of being in the sea amidst the large breakers; I could never understand what my father meant. In my memory, that my mother and sister were sitting on the beach and not playing in the water, seems both accurate and appropriate. My sister was shy and quiet; very much her mother's girl. My mother was not given to boisterous behaviour or outbursts of laughter; she seemed to bear her husband's teasing with a certain amount of resignation. The photographs show my mother and me together only occasionally, and then, quiet and subdued.

My mother looked after us, working hard at home. She spent a lot of time thinking about food, buying it and preparing it: but not a lot of time eating it. Mealtimes were very important for the family; we would always eat round a square wooden table. Always at the same time, on the dot. The menu was unvaried; each day was different but each week was the same.

There were other memories from my childhood. They were not like the ones stored on the photographs, they were not happy, nor contained; they were sad and vivid. They needed no evocation. They were part of myself that I could command as surely as I could summon the memory of the pleasant evening I spent last night.

When I was four, I had my tonsils out. I remember it vividly, being in hospital. A nurse trying to make me eat tomato soup (something which we never ate at home and made me think of blood), and jelly and custard together, which I hated and my mother would never have given me. I can remember being assured of lots of ice-cream before I went in; but I can't remember ever getting it. I remember being frightened and lonely and wanting my mummy to be there. It was the days before mums and dads stayed with their children in hospital.

I had just started school when my grandmother died suddenly, although not unexpectedly, if that is possible. My mother, whose mother it was, was distraught at the time, and depressed for a long time afterwards. It was a traumatic time for everyone. It remains vivid in my memory. I had returned from school for my lunch and had found my mother sitting crying on the sofa. A kindly neighbour brought me into the kitchen/dining-room where I had my lunch as usual – it was sausages, potatoes and peas. I will never forget it. My grandmother was kept at home, as was traditional, and she was placed, in her coffin, in the kitchen/dining-room, where the food was still prepared but now no longer eaten. I was taken away for the funeral itself though I had stayed for the whole of the lying in. I am told that I used to 'play' with my dead grandmother, pulling out her eyebrows and combing her hair. When my aunt arrived I said, 'Come and look, auntie, the coffin's got pretty little handles.' It is intimated, although never stated directly, that my behaviour caused distress and was considered to be, at some level, callous.

Things seemed to change after my grandmother's death. My mother was very sad and didn't want to go out. I wanted to go to dance classes. She took me, and to elocution, too. I didn't like that as much. I loved dancing, passionately. I would dance in the street and the neighbours would nudge each other and whisper to my mother that I was 'out there again'. I would dance in the house, flinging myself from chair to chair, pirouetting, jumping, landing with a 'dying fall'. I didn't care. I loved dancing classes; I was good, too. I was chosen to be part of a special chorus at the end of year show. When it came to enrol again, my mother didn't enrol me for dancing classes. She did for elocution. It was what she wanted and what she could afford. I was desperately unhappy; most of all I wanted to dance. At my elocution lessons was another girl, my mother's friend's daughter. We were the same age, at the same school, in the same class. I hated her. My mother often commented, 'I don't know why you can't be like her, she is so neat and tidy and polite and charming.' I would reply, 'If you want her so badly, why don't you have her instead of me?' Now we were in elocution together and no doubt, she spoke nicer, too.

However, I did do well, winning prizes at competitions. But it wasn't the same. Later, I learned that my mother hadn't taken me to dancing classes because it meant meeting other mothers on her own and she couldn't face that. But somehow I could never forgive her for denying me the chance to express my spirit with my body; to celebrate my body's strength and grace. But most of all, I could never forgive her for not giving me the choice.

Meanwhile, at school I did well, but not too well. I liked school, but I liked playing and dreaming better. There was no doubt that I would go to a grammar school, there was never any doubt, ever. I was as bright as a button. Being bright meant going to a school many miles away. No one else chose the school that I wanted to go to, they went to all-girls' schools (no boys passed the 11 plus). So, at the age of ten, when I passed the 11 plus, I began to feel my isolation and loneliness.

Going to grammar school was a major event in my life. My mother tells me that I left home then, when I was just eleven. I can remember the uniform, slightly too big and brand, spanking new. I can remember going to buy it; the anxiety about getting it right and how much it cost. I can remember the grey socks and my ugly, round-toed shoes. It took two buses to take me to school. On that first day my mother rode with me to the second bus stop, in town. We were both anxious. On that second bus, with lots of children going to the same school, two second years asked me my name, and laughed at it and gave me a nickname, which stayed with me until I was grown up. I was scared of my new school but I met a friend in the first five minutes: she stayed with me, too.

I was popular with my teachers – my form teacher especially. I shone, my friend told me later: my skin shone, my eyes shone, my hair shone, my smile beamed from ear to ear. I had lots of energy and enthusiasm: sheer, forceful enthusiasm, apparently unaware of the suspicion that such behaviour arouses in peers. I was myself and I was lively. There were indications of insecurity then, at the age of eleven. I had a pretend dog, and a pretend glamorous sister with a glamorous name. They had to be got rid of when my friend came home for the first time. The agony of being found out. During my first year I was a success; my best subjects were Maths and French. By the beginning of my third year I was not doing as well, not dramatically, but perceptibly. My periods had started and I had kissed my first boy. Things began to change.

I started to want privacy – to have my own thoughts and feelings. But there was no space at home – neither physically nor emotionally. On Saturday mornings my parents always went out shopping: my sister, who was almost married would, inevitably, be out. I used to go out with my parents. Now, I wanted desperately to be on my own, in my own room, left with my own, now growing and changing body. I would lie in bed, in the quietness, and touch my body and explore it and smell my smells. It was totally fascinating; I started to experience sensations that both frightened and excited me. I didn't know what any of it meant. I was confused and, perhaps, alarmed. Certainly, I had started to become alarming to my parents.

One evening I went out with my only friend on my side of town. My friend went to the secondary modern school; she didn't have to do homework, she could stay out late, she had brothers who were almost men. We went to a gymnastics display and on the way home we got chatting to two boys. They flirted and we flirted back. By the town hall, he kissed me and I kissed him back. I had never felt like that before; I wanted to go on kissing until my breath stopped. He kissed me on the neck and bit me, violently, passionately; I adored it. My friend had to drag me away and we leapt on the same bus. I walked down the street oblivious of everything except myself: unaware of the time and unaware that my parents might be worried. They were waiting for me anxiously, and when I got to the front gate my father shouted at me and my mother cried. I went straight to bed. My father said that I wasn't allowed out for a month. When I got to bed, I showed my sister my 'love-bites' and she looked worried. It made me worry, and I went downstairs early the next morning and put some make-up on them. When my mother got up the next day I told her about what had happened and showed her my neck. Again, my mother cried, and called me 'my baby'. The next day at school, a girl in my form said to me, 'You mean you let a boy kiss you and you don't even wear a bra.' I can remember feeling ashamed but I didn't really know why.

And so the battles really began. I stopped going to church. My father had taken me every Sunday morning since I had been small. The church was austere and cold. The minister would tell us that we had puny little minds that could hardly grasp God's wonder and that we were worthless without his love. As I grew older I began to hate them all, their hypocrisy and their own pious and judgemental attitudes. Almost the last time I went I wore nylons without my mother knowing: when she found out she was cross. My mother wanted me to wear ankle socks. There would be time enough to be a grown woman. People at church asked her why I had stopped going. I had stopped because I didn't believe in God. My mother defended me to them, saying, 'She will never do anything that will make me hang my head in shame.'

Going to church was one of the few, remaining things that I did with my father. When I stopped going, we stopped having those walks together to and from; and the inevitable conversations. Perhaps we stopped talking altogether.

I started to wear odd clothes; from jumble sales and of my own making. And make-up – strange make-up – white or black lips; dark, violent-coloured eyelids. I plucked my eyebrows away and back-combed my hair. My mother was outraged and she shouted at me; she wouldn't let me out looking like that; so I removed it all and put it on again on the bus. And it was all a façade: underneath I was scared and lonely but I desperately wanted to be myself, to define who I was, to express my very nature. I couldn't find the words so I used my body, my face. I looked to photographs in magazines: there the girls were beautiful and thin. I liked that gaunt, yet childlike appearance. They seemed to express something that I felt. Yet I wasn't thin and I wanted to be. I stopped eating, not dramatically, but little by little. I became a vegetarian and my mother fussed. I lost weight. My mother took me to the doctor who tried to persuade me to eat fish, at least. So I did.

In the cold early mornings it was worst. My mother would try to get me to eat porridge for breakfast: I would refuse and we would sit together – me hating my mother, wanting her to go away; hating this early morning intimacy; hating being watched, being seen by this person who could see into the very inside of me. I would sit, stonily, rejecting my mother and my food, and feeling so bad that I would storm out of the house, banging the door and the gate.

In the end it was my mother who broke down. We were having lunch with my sister; my mother began to cry, 'What have I done, why doesn't she speak to me, what can I do?' I felt victorious, but empty. It was so through the last school years: silent battles with my mother; raging, stormy ones with myself.

At school the picture was blurred. I did reasonably well in my exams. I wanted to stay on for A-levels, and did. Those last two years were spent in a haze of despair and depression. I related badly to my peers; I wanted to be beautiful but considered myself not to be; I had my friend but we were in different groups and besides, she had a boyfriend. I was alone and felt lonely. I read poetry; I treasured Keats, 'And now more than ever it seemed rich to die, to cease upon the midnight with no pain.' He expressed my anguish for me. I felt unloved. In my worst moments I even cried, and in the midst of my sobs, were the words 'nobody loves me' expressed over and over again. Towards the end of my school years I discovered T.S. Eliot and I carried his poems around with me. He seemed to know how I felt, too, 'What shall I do now? What shall I do? I shall rush out as I am, and walk the street with my hair down, so. What shall we do tomorrow? What shall we ever do?'

I described my life through the words of others. I had no voice of my own. And in the end, it wasn't just that I felt unloved, but I felt unlovable. I could change my appearance to make it more acceptable, more attractive, more lovable, but underneath, there was nothing that could be done to rescue me from my own ugliness.

I left school to go to college. I didn't really know what I wanted to do: helping others was the only thing that inspired me. The college wasn't too far away from home. Strangely, I didn't want to go too far away from my parents. I was unhappy, but somehow or other, decisions about my life, whilst I was at college, didn't have to be taken. I could avoid responsibilities. When I left college and got my first job I had to face up to those decisions, accept the responsibility for my own life. The autonomy that had been so fiercely fought for was now powerfully threatening. I started to read, voraciously; I could not have enough. As if I was searching for meaning, for identity, for an explanation, for a way of being that could be loved. I met a young man who fell in love with me and I had my first real sexual experience. I felt passionate about him and yet, almost immediately, frightened of and controlled by my desire: as though it would devour and destroy him. Eventually, I hated myself, and him. He was dismayed at first and then, angry. He didn't understand me. I became ill. I was taken into hospital to have my appendix out. When I came out of hospital I had lost weight.

Two months after the operation I went to a party. There I met an old colleague. He remarked on my weight loss and said that I suited it; in fact, he said, I looked much more attractive. I reduced my intake of food, considerably, from that moment on. I stopped eating potatoes and bread; then butter and cheese. I started to 'eat up' all the information I could get about calories; I read diet books with consuming interest. My food was weighed; measured according to calorific value. I grew very thin indeed. I felt good; enjoyed my thinness, my protruding hip bones, my bony shoulders. I felt acceptable and worthy. When I went out with friends for a drink, I would panic if the pub didn't sell low calorie drinks. I felt that food was poisoning me; that to eat and drink normally would, literally, kill me. Soon, I was eating fruit and dry crispbreads, lettuce and celery and a little, very lean meat. My diet was unvaried. Every day had to be the same. I panicked if the shop did not have exactly the brand of crispbread I wanted; I panicked if I could not eat, ritually, at the same time. I controlled exactly what I was eating; I was safe from the dangerous world of living and eating – but I was unhappy and desperately lonely. Along with my control of food and my inability to eat (it *was* impossible for me to eat), came the difficulty in being with people, too. I was constantly hungry, I could not concentrate on what anyone was saying or doing. I joined evening classes in order that I might make new friends; but I could not sustain them. By eight o'clock I would be so hungry that I could think of nothing but food. I was too hungry even to read, one thing that might have given me some comfort. Sometimes, it would all become so overwhelming that I would eat voraciously. At parties I would take food, putting it in my handbag and taking it home. Sometimes I would eat a little of it, but more often than not, I would be so overwhelmed with guilt about having taken it, that I would throw it out.

Some people were kind and tried to look after me, bringing me healthy foods, for my cover was health food. But they would soon disappear, unable to cope with my distress. Women especially, were drawn to me, envying my slenderness. I liked to boast that I had no problems with my weight; that I could eat anything I wanted; that I really enjoyed cottage cheese and lettuce. I knew that I could do what most people couldn't do; it didn't make me feel any better.

I began to feel ill; to be aware that there was something quite wrong with me. I went to the doctor and explained that I couldn't eat and that I was worried that I might die. The doctor referred me to the hospital.

I went for the appointed time; I was, in fact, very early. I looked around the waiting room. There were people there who were really ill – old and demented. All of them were poor. I was frightened by them; frightened of being one of them. I started to panic; I wanted to run away. But I stayed and waited until the doctor came.

The doctor had a kind, understanding face; tall but not thin. I was, somehow, reassured by her size and her shape. She asked me about myself; my likes, my dislikes, my ambitions. She wanted to know about my family, about my job. She asked me about my weight; she didn't seem unduly concerned. She wanted to know about me. On subsequent visits, she did weigh me, to make sure my weight was stable, but I never felt that it was that important. How I felt about my body was important; what it meant to be thin was important; having a relationship where I felt accepted for what I was was important – 'Somehow being seen for what one was made up for the misery of being it.'

Just at the time of starting to see the doctor regularly, I saw my mother and father. It was a terrible time for me, and for them. It was my mother who visited first. She was visibly shocked by my appearance and obviously alarmed. Throughout the evening we tried to talk and she tried to entice me with my favourite foods. I refused everything. The next morning my mother came into my room with a cup of tea for me; she tried to embrace me, to hold me in her arms like a small child, to comfort me in the way she had done so many times before in the past. But it was no use. 'Go away, please leave me alone.' My bony body turned away from her, my sobs silent. 'Please let me help you, please,' she pleaded, weeping herself. But it was no good at all. She left, defeated and rejected.

I went home soon after my mother's visit. It was my summer holiday. I was very, very nervous. My father had not seen me thin. No doubt my mother had told him, prepared him, but I knew that he would be shocked. He was. He said nothing; afterwards, I learned that he had gone to see my sister later that same day and broken down. 'She used to be so bonny,' he had said. He had lost his little girl. The family was devastated. Mealtimes were agony. My father could hardly resist commenting on my tiny plate of food, and my mother fretted, anxiously eating her own food, and patently upset about me. She made all the things I used to eat, but I could not eat them, I could not put them in my mouth. I was, no longer, actively resisting my mother; it was as though I had been taken over. There were no rows, now, no arguments; no one dared to argue or disagree, just in case I cracked, so frail did I seem.

Of course I was frail, but I also perceived myself as being very strong, as being indestructible. During that summer holiday spent at home, I began to feel a bit better. Throughout the winter that followed, however, my life was grim. I became aware that I was inexpressibly miserable and indescribably hungry. I began to know, with the help of my doctor, that I needn't be miserable and hungry. That there was another way. It was not easy though.

The process of eating began by drinking white wine. My doctor said that it was believed that 'the super-ego was soluble in alcohol'. After two glasses of white wine, I would begin to be able to eat; as though my iron will had been melted, the furnace fuelled by the alcohol. I would eat in a crazy, chaotic way; stuffing food into my mouth like a starving creature. After I had eaten like that, I would feel guilty and deprive myself for a day or so.

The chaos was terrifying; I felt as though I might lose myself; that I would gorge myself until I split at the seams. But I began to recognise, slowly, that eating also felt good. More and more often I began to eat; not in a regular way but, in my own sporadic way, I began to enjoy it.

Perhaps I would have gone on like that for a long time. My doctor certainly felt that I was much better. I had been seeing her for almost a year. Every Friday. Together, we had explored my feelings about my parents; my confusion about who I was and who I wanted to be. I trusted her. I needed her; this person who listened so carefully to what I said, who didn't judge me, who didn't tell me what to do, who let me be. I tried, with her help, to unravel the tangle of my confusing and conflicting emotions.

But in the end it was up to me. It was so hard to accept. She would help me but she couldn't tell me how to live. It was my life, after all. It belonged to me; I could cultivate it; I could nourish it or I could starve it. I could choose. It was such a burden, that choice, that sometimes I thought I could not bear it on my own. Reluctantly, I stopped going to see her, and I missed her. She referred me to a group and I went for a while, but I didn't really like it, so I stopped.

One day, quite by chance, I met one of my neighbours. I had been living in a flat, in a street, throughout this time. I realised that I knew no one there. She lived alone with her young son. Gradually, I got to know them. She was very open, warm and friendly. I was able to talk to her, to tell her about myself and, eventually, to laugh with her. I often would visit her after work. She would be preparing food for her son and I would watch. I began to experience how people ate and how much they ate; I began to learn how to eat myself.

There were other friends. My school friend and I still spent time together. We had been friends for so long that we could relax with each other; we could leave sentences half finished. A colleague from work lived nearby and I began to see her and her husband. They had a warm and welcoming home and there was always food around. It was good to be with them for they were generous and accepting.

I joined the local community centre and I became quite involved in some of the campaigns. It gave me a focus; something to do at night, and during the weekends, which were the worst times. I soon realised that I could become involved, participate and even organise. I felt good.

Two years after it all began, I was still thin, still anxious about food, still restraining my appetite, still ignoring my hunger (as though to admit to hunger would be to admit to having needs). But it was bearable. I could relax, I could enjoy being with people and give something to them, I could concentrate and think and begin to be creative again.

That Christmas, when I was feeling better, I went to a party where I met a friend of a friend. He was warm and full of humour. He made me laugh, he held me and I felt good and safe. He wanted to see me again; placing his hands on my shoulders, he said that he wanted to see me again. I was amazed. I did see him again, and again. He so obviously wanted me that I couldn't help but respond. I began to express my own longing and desire for him; my hunger for him when he was absent. And it was good. It did not destroy him, it enriched him: it did not devour him, it made him more whole. Through our relationship I felt secure enough, accepted enough to eat. I did eat, not huge meals, but regularly and with enjoyment.

Our relationship was the final part of the process; something that had begun several years before. So many people had been involved, and each had helped me in their own way.

The end of the story is really, of course, the beginning. I had always thought that there was an answer; that someone knew how to live without pain and anxiety. I discovered that finding answers, learning how to live, was, by definition, painful, but something that I could no longer do alone. I was more vulnerable than before, for I was not shielded by my thinness and my sadness any more. It is a risky business, being a woman. I have found different strategies to cope; ones that are under my control. The struggle to be myself, autonomous and free, goes on.

Notes

Preface: pages 3–6

1. Cooper, Troy, 'Anorexia and Bulimia: The Political and the Personal', in Lawrence, M. (ed), *Fed Up and Hungry*, The Women's Press, 1987.

2. Lawrence, M., 'Education and Identity: The Social Origins of Anorexia', in Lawrence, M. (ed), *Fed Up and Hungry*, The Women's Press, 1987.

3. Lask, B. and Bryant Waugh, R., 'Early-onset Anorexia Nervosa and Related Eating Disorders', *Journal of Child Psychology and Psychiatry*, Vol. 33, no. 1, pp. 281–300, 1992.

4. Oppenheimer, R., Howels, K., Palmer, R. L and Chaloner D.A., 'Adverse sexual experience in childhood and clinical eating disorders: A preliminary description', in Szmukler, G., Slade, P. et al (eds), *Anorexia Nervosa and Bulimic Disorders*, Pergamon Press, 1986.

Chapter 1: pages 15–26

1. I have borrowed the idea of the true and false self from the child analyst D. W. Winnicott. Winnicott, D.W., 'Ego Distortion in Terms of True and False Self' in *The Maturational Processes and the Facilitating Environment*, Hogarth Press, London, 1965.

2. MacLeod, S., *The Art of Starvation*, Virago, London, 1981.

Chapter 2: pages 27–42

1. E.g. Palmer, R.L., *Anorexia Nervosa*, Penguin, London, 1980.

2. This is fully discussed in the pamphlet *Food and Profit*, produced

by the Politics of Health Group, printed by Blackrose Press, 30 Clerkenwell Close, London EC1.

3. Ehrenreich, B. and English, D., *For Her Own Good*, Anchor Press, New York, 1978.

4. Davin, A., 'Imperialism and Motherhood', *History Workshop 5*, Routledge and Kegan Paul, London, 1978, pp. 9–65

5. Bruch, H., *Eating Disorders*, Routledge and Kegan Paul, London, 1974.

6. Lawrence, M., 'Anorexia Nervosa: The Control Paradox', *Women's Studies*, Vol. 2, no. 1, 1979, pp. 93–101.

7. Mensching, G., *Structures and Patterns of Religion*, translated by Klimheit, H.F. and Sharma, S., Banarsidass, Delhi, 1976.

8. Douglas, M., *Purity and Danger*, Routledge and Kegan Paul, London, 1966.

9. Chamberlain, M., *Old Wives' Tales*, Virago, London, 1981.

10. Bruch, H., *Eating Disorders*, Routledge and Kegan Paul, London, 1974.

11. MacLeod, S., *The Art of Starvation*, Virago, London, 1981.

12. Huxley, A., *Chrome Yellow*, Chatto and Windus, London, 1958.

13. Ehrenreich, B. and English, D., op. cit.

14. Ehrenreich, B. and English, D., op. cit., p. 93. 'Doctors found a variety of diagnostic labels for the wave of invalidism gripping the female population: "neurasthenia", "nervous prostration", "hyperesthesia", "cardiac inadequacy", "dyspepsia", "rheumatism", and "hysteria". The symptoms included headache, muscular aches, weakness, depression, menstrual difficulties, indigestion etc., and usually a general debility requiring constant rest.'

15. Chernin, K., *Womanize*, The Women's Press, London, 1983.

16. Wooley, O.W., Wooley, S.C. and Dyrenforth, S.R., 'Obesity and Women II: A Neglected Feminist Topic', *Women's Studies*, Vol. 2, no. 1, 1979, pp. 81–92.

17. Monello, L. F. and Mayer, J., 'Obese Adolescent Girls: An Unrecognised "Minority" Group?', *American Journal of Clinical Nutrition*, 13, 1963, 35–39.

18. Orbach, S., *Fat is a Feminist Issue*, Paddington Press, London, 1978.

19. Garrow, J., 'Energy Balance and Obesity in Man', American

Elsevier, 1974, cited by Wooley, O.W. and Wooley, S.C. in 'Obesity and Women I: A Closer Look at the Facts', *Women's Studies*, Vol. 2, no. 1, 1979.

20. Goodman, N., Dornbusch, S.M., Richardson, S. A. and Hastorf, A. H., 'Variant Reactions to Physical Disabilities', *American Sociology Review*, 28, 429–435, cited by Wooley, O.W., Wooley, S.C. and Dyrenforth, S.R., op cit.

A. H., 'Variant Reactions to Physical Disabilities', *American Sociology Review*, 28, 429–435, cited by Wooley, O.W., Wooley, S.C. and Dyrenforth, S.R., op. cit.

21. Contento, I., 'The Nutritional Needs of Women', in Kaplan, J.R. (ed), *A Woman's Conflict: The Special Relationship Between Women and Food*, Prentice Hall, New York, 1980.

22. Wooley, O. W. and Wooley, S.C., op. cit.

23. Davis, A., *Let's Get Well*, George Allen and Unwin, London, 1966.

Chapter 3: pages 43–55

1. Brown, G. and Harris, T., *Social Origins of Depression*, Tavistock, London, 1978.

2. Palmer, R.L., *Anorexia Nervosa*, Penguin, London, 1980.

3. Waller, J. V., Kaufman, R. and Deutsch, F., 'Anorexia Nervosa: A Psychosomatic Entity', *Psychosomatic Medicine*, 2, 1940, 3–16.

4. Dally, P. and Gomez, J., *Anorexia Nervosa*, Heinemann, London, 1979.

5. Palmer, R. L., op. cit.

6. Dally, P. and Gomez, J., op. cit.

7. Williams, J.H., *Psychology of Women*, Norton, New York and London, 1974.

8. Spender, D., *Invisible Women*, Writers and Readers Publishing Co-operative, London, 1982.

Chapter 4: pages 56–74

1. Lambley, P., *How to Survive Anorexia*, Frederick Muller, London, 1983.

2. Lambley, P., op. cit.

3. Lambley, P., op. cit.

4. Lambley, P. op. cit.

5. Bruch, H., *Eating Disorders*, Routledge and Kegan Paul, London, 1974.

6. Winnicott, D.W., 'The Theory of the Parent-Infant Relationship' (1960) in *The Maturational Processes and the Facilitating Environment*, Hogarth Press, London, 1965.

7. The term 'castrate' which Winnicott uses on p.51 is clearly an odd word to use with reference to girl-children. It is of course a good example of the tendency of writers to assume, at least implicitly, that all children are male. He means 'to make powerless'.

8. Winnicott, D. W., op. cit., p. 52.

9. Bruch, H., op. cit.

10. Minuchin, S., Rosman, B. L. Baker, L., *Psychosomatic Families*, Harvard University Press, Cambridge, Massachusetts, and London, 1978.

11. MacLeod, S., *The Art of Starvation*, Virago, London, 1981.

12. Minuchin, S. et al, op. cit.

13. Flax, J., 'The Conflict Between Nurturance and Autonomy', in Howel, E. and Bayes, M. (eds), *Women and Mental Health*, Basic Books, New York, 1981.

14. Flax, J., op. cit.

Chapter 5: pages 75–90

1. Bruch, H., *The Golden Cage: The Enigma of Anorexia Nervosa*, Open Books, London, 1978.

2. Palmer, R. L., *Anorexia Nervosa*, Penguin, London, 1980.

3. Crisp, A. H., *Let Me Be*, London University Press, 1980.

4. Bruch, H., op. cit.

5. Bruch, H., op. cit.

6. Gull, W. W., 'Anorexia Nervosa', *Transactions of the Clinical Society*, London, 7, 1874, 22–28.

7. Bruch, H., 'Perils of Behaviour Modification in the Treatment of Anorexia Nervosa', *Journal of the American Medical Association*, 230, 1974, 1419–22.

Chapter 6: pages 91–109

1. Lawrence, M., 'Anorexia Nervosa: The Counsellor's Role', *British Journal of Guidance and Counselling*, Vol. 9, no. 1, Jan 1981, pp. 74–85.

2. Bruch, H., *The Golden Cage: The Enigma of Anorexia Nervosa*, Open Books, London, 1978.

3. Lawrence, M., op. cit.

4. Hilde Bruch, in the final chapter of *The Golden Cage*, describes this very well.

5. D. W. Winnicott intriguingly alludes to this process in 'Communicating and Not Communicating Leading to a Study of Certain Opposites' (1963) in *The Maturational Process and the Facilitating Environment*, Hogarth Press, London, 1965.

6. Palmer, R. L., *Anorexia Nervosa*, Penguin, London, 1980.

7. MacLeod, S., *The Art of Starvation*, Virago, London, 1981.

Bibliography

Aronoff, J., 'Sex Differences in the Orientation of Body Image', *Journal of Personality Assessment*, 36, 1972, 19–22.

Askevold, F., 'Measuring Body Image: Preliminary Report on a New Method', *Psychotherapy and Psychosomatics*, 26, 1975, 71–7.

Binswanger, L., 'Der Fall Ellen West', *Archiv für Neurologie und Psychiatrie*, 53: 255–77; 54: 69–117, 330–60; 55: 16–40, 1944, trans. Mendel, W. and Lyons, J. in May, R., Angel, E. and Ellenberger, H. (eds), *Existence*, Basic Books, New York, 1958.

Birksted-Breen, D., 'Working with an Anorexic Patient', *International Journal of Psychoanalysis*, 70, 1989, 29–40.

Boskind-Lodahl, M., 'Cinderella's Step-Sisters: A Feminist Perspective on Anorexia Nervosa and Bulimia', in Howell, E. and Bayes, M., *Women and Mental Health*, Basic Books, New York, 1981.

Bruch, H., *Eating Disorders: Obesity, Anorexia Nervosa and the Person Within*, Routledge and Kegan Paul, London, 1974.

Bruch, H., *The Golden Cage: The Engima of Anorexia Nervosa*, Open Books, London, 1978.

Bruch, H., 'Perceptual and Conceptual Disturbances in Anorexia Nervosa', *Psychosomatic Medicine*, 24, 1962, 187–94.

Bruch, H., 'Death in Anorexia Nervosa', *Psychosomatic Medicine*, 33, 1971, 135–44.

Bruch, H., 'Anorexia Nervosa in the Male', *Psychosomatic Medicine*, 33, 1971, 135–44.

Bruch, H., 'Psychotherapy in Primary Anorexia Nervosa', *Journal of Nervous and Mental Disorders*, 150, 1970, 51–67.

Bruch, H., 'Perils of Behaviour Modification in the Treatment of

Anorexia Nervosa', *Journal of the American Medical Association*, 230, 1974, 1419–22.

Bruch, H., 'Obesity and Anorexia Nervosa: Psychological Aspects', *Australian and New Zealand Journal of Psychiatry*, 2(3), 1975, 159–61.

Brunberg, J., *Fasting Girls*, Harvard University Press, Cambridge, Massachusetts, 1988.

Button, E. J., Fransella, F. and Slade, P. D., 'A Re-appraisal of Body Perception Disturbance in Anorexia Nervosa', *Psychological Medicine*, 7, 1977, 235–43.

Chernin, K., *Womansize: The Tyranny of Slenderness*, The Women's Press, London, 1983.

Chernin, K., *The Hungry Self: Women, Eating and Identity*, Virago, London, 1986.

Crisp, A.H., *Anorexia Nervosa: Let Me Be*, Academic Press, London 1980.

Crisp, A. H., 'A Treatment Regime for Anorexia Nervosa', *British Journal of Psychiatry*, 112, 1965, 505–12.

Crisp, A. H. and Toms, D. A., 'Primary Anorexia Nervosa or Weight Phobia in the Male', *British Medical Journal*, 1, 1972, 334–38.

Crisp, A.H., Harding, B. and McGuiness, B., 'Anorexia Nervosa: Psychoneurotic Characteristics of Parents: Relationship to Prognosis. A Quantitative Study', *Journal of Psychosomatic Research*, 18, 1974, 167–73.

Crisp, A.H., Palmer, R.L. and Kalucy, R.S., 'How Common is Anorexia Nervosa? A Prevalence Study', *British Journal of Psychiatry*, 128, 1976, 549–54.

Dally, P., *Anorexia Nervosa*, Grune and Stratton, New York, 1969.

Dally, P. and Gomez, J., *Anorexia Nervosa*, Heinemann, London, 1979.

Dana, M. and Lawrence, M., *Women's Secret Disorder: A New Understanding of Bulimia*, Grafton, London, 1988.

Dolan, B. and Gitzinger, I. (eds), *Why Women? Gender Issues and Eating Disorders*, Athlone Press, London, 1994.

Fisher, S. and Cleveland, S.E., *Body Image and Personality*, Dover Publications, New York, 1968.

Garfinkel, P.E., Kline, S.A. and Stancer, A.C., 'Treatment of

Anorexia Nervosa Using Operant Conditioning Techniques', *Journal of Nervous and Mental Diseases*, 6, 1973, 428–33.

Gull, W.W., 'Anorexia Nervosa (Apepsia Hysterica, Anorexia Hysterica)', *Transactions of the Clinical Society* (London), 7, 1874, 22.

Hus, L. K. G., Meltzer, E. S. and Crisp, A. H. 'Schizophrenia and Anorexia Nervosa', *Transactions of the Clinical Society* (London), 7, 1874, 22.

Hus, L. K. G., Meltzer, E. S. and Crisp, A. H., 'Schizophrenia and Anorexia Nervosa', *Journal of Nervous and Mental Diseases*, 169, 1981, 273–6.

Kalucy, R. S., Crisp, A.H. and Harding, B., 'A Study of Fifty-Six Families with Anorexia Nervosa', *British Journal of Psychology*, 50, 1977, 381–95.

Lasegue, C., 'On Hysterical Anorexia', *Medical Times and Gazette*, 2, 1873, 265–6, 367–9.

Lawrence, M., 'Anorexia Nervosa: The Control Paradox', *Women's Studies International Quarterly*, 2, 1979, 93–101.

Lawrence, M., 'Anorexia Nervosa: The Counsellor's Role', *British Journal of Guidance and Counselling*, 9, 1981, 74–85.

Lawrence, M., 'Education and Identity: Thoughts on the Social Origins of Anorexia', *Women's Studies International Forum*, Vol. 7, no. 4, 1984, 201–10.

Lawrence, M. (ed.), *Fed Up and Hungry: Women, Oppression and Food*, The Women's Press, London, 1987.

MacLeod, S., *The Art of Starvation*, Virago, London, 1981.

Meyer, J.E., 'Anorexia Nervosa of Adolescence: The Central Syndrome of the Anorexia Nervosa Group', *British Journal of Psychiatry*, 118, 1971, 539–42.

Minuchin, S., Rosman, B.L. and Baker, L., *Psychosomatic Families: Anorexia Nervosa in Context*, Harvard University Press, Cambridge, Massachusetts, 1978.

Moorey, J., *Living with Anorexia and Bulimia*, Manchester University Press, Manchester, 1991.

Morgan, H.G., 'Fasting Girls and our Attitudes to Them', *British Medical Journal*, 2, 1977, 1652–55.

Orbach, S., *Fat is a Feminist Issue*, Hamlyn, London, 1979.

Orbach, S., *Hunger Strike*, Faber, London, 1986.

Palmer, R.L., *Anorexia Nervosa*, Penguin, London, 1980.

Palmer, R.L., 'Dietary Chaos Syndrome: A Useful New Term?', *British Journal of Medical Psychology*, 52, 1979, 187–90.

Pillay, M. and Crisp, A.H., 'Some Psychological Characteristics of Patients with Anorexia Nervosa, Whose Weight has been Newly Restored', *British Journal of Medical Psychology*, 50, 1977, 375–80.

Russell, G. F. M., 'Bulimia Nervosa: An Ominous Variant of Anorexia Nervosa', *Psychological Medicine*, 9, 1979, 429–48.

Russell, G. F. M., 'The Nutritional Disorder in Anorexia Nervosa', *Journal of Psychosomatic Research*, 134, 1979, 60–6.

Selvini-Palazzoli, M., *Self Starvation*, Chaucer Publishing House, London, 1974.

Sohn, L., 'Anorexic and bulimic states of mind in the psychoanalytic treatment of anorexic/bulimic patients and psychotic patients', *Psychoanalysis, Psychotherapy*, 1, 1985, 49–56.

Stunkard, A. and Burt, V., 'Obesity and the Body Image II: Age at Onset of Disturbances in the Body Image', *American Journal of Psychiatry*, 123, 1967, 1443–47.

Thomas, H., *Anorexia Nervosa*, Huber-Klett, Bern-Stuttgart, 1961; International University Press, New York, 1967.

Vandereycken, W. and Van Deth, R., *From Fasting Saints to Anorexic Girls*, Athlone Press, London, 1994.

Waller, J.V., Kaufman, R. and Deutsch, F., 'Anorexia Nervosa. A Psychosomatic Entity', *Psychosomatic Medicine*, 2, 1940, 3–16.

Wilson, C. P., Hogan, C. C. and Mintz, I. L., *Psycho-dynamic Technique in the Treatment of the Eating Disorders*, Jason Aronson, London, 1992.

Yager, J., 'Family Issues in the Pathogenesis of Anorexia Nervosa', *Psychosomatic Medicine*, 44, 1982, 43–60.

Resources

Eating Disorders Association

First Floor, Wensum House, 103 Prince of Wales Road,
Norwich, Norfolk NR1 1DW

Eating Disorders Association is a self-help organisation committed to forging links between those who suffer from anorexia or bulimia and those who try to help. EDA supports a national network of self-help groups and publishes regular newsletters. They can also help with information about local resources and are very concerned to provide help for parents and other carers as well as sufferers.

Telephone Helplines 01603 621414 (Mon–Fri, 9am–6.30pm)
Youth Helpline (18 yrs and under) 01603 765050 (Mon–Fri, 4–6pm)

If you would like to listen to a recorded message (approx 10 minutes) about anorexia nervosa and bulimia, call 0891 615466 (50p per minute).

The Women's Therapy Centre

6 Manor Gardens, London N7

The Women's Therapy Centre has a great deal of experience in helping women with eating disorders. Write for information about groups and workshops.

Index

The Women's Press is Britain's leading women's publishing house. Established in 1978, we publish high-quality fiction and non-fiction from outstanding women writers worldwide. Our exciting and diverse list includes literary fiction, detective novels, biography and autobiography, health, women's studies, handbooks, literary criticism, psychology and self-help, the arts, our popular Livewire Books series for young women and the bestselling annual *Women Artists Diary* featuring beautiful colour and black-and-white illustrations from the best in contemporary women's art.

If you would like more information about our books or about our mail order book club, please send an A5 sae for our latest catalogue and complete list to:

The Sales Department
The Women's Press Ltd
34 Great Sutton Street
London EC1V 0DX
Tel: 0171 251 3007
Fax: 0171 608 1938

Also of interest:

Marilyn Lawrence, editor
Fed Up and Hungry
Women, Oppression and Food

With a foreword by Susie Orbach

Why does food cause women so much stress? Why can we not just feed ourselves and be done with it? What is it that makes so many women in the West preoccupied with their weight and dissatisfied with their bodies? What is the meaning of so-called 'eating disorders'?

In this stimulating and positive collection of essays, women who have direct experience – personal or professional – of 'eating disorders' analyse the complex social forces which affect our relationship with our bodies. Exploring the realities of anorexia nervosa, bulimia and our compulsive eating, they offer vital possibilities for positive change in our attitudes to food and to ourselves.

Psychology/Women Studies £7.99
ISBN 0 7043 4008 9

The Women's Press Handbook Series

Kathy Nairne and Gerrilyn Smith
Dealing with Depression

Second Edition – Fully revised and updated

Why do so many women suffer from depression?
How can we defend ourselves against this common
problem and get out of what can quickly become a
vicious circle?

Kathy Nairne and Gerrilyn Smith, both clinical
psychologists, draw on their extensive professional
experience together with the experiences of a wide
range of women sufferers to offer this down-to-earth
and comprehensive guide. From identifying the
causes of depression to understanding the many
forms it can take, from different ways of coping and
recovering to evaluating the help available, here is an
essential handbook for anyone who has experienced
depression, either in themselves or others.

**'A straightforward, practical guide...it explores its
subject in depth.'** *Company*

**'I can thoroughly recommend this practical,
sympathetic and non-patronising book.'**
London Newspaper Group

Health/Self Help £6.99
ISBN 0 7043 4443 2

The Women's Press Handbook Series

Valerie Hey, Catherine Itzin, Lesley
Saunders and Mary Ann Speakman, editors
Hidden Loss
Miscarriage and Ectopic Pregnancy

Why is the reality of a pre-birth loss so often hidden
by euphemisms or evasions? Why can it be so
difficult for us to grieve over a miscarriage or ectopic
pregnancy?

One in five pregnancies fail – yet miscarriage remains
a footnote in most pregnancy books, its emotional and
physical impact minimised. Now, this vitally
important and urgently needed handbook draws on
women's personal accounts to fully explore the
experience of pre-birth loss. Finally recognising
miscarriage and ectopic pregnancy as bereavements,
Hidden Loss offers a thorough understanding of the
experience of mourning, discusses self-help
techniques to aid the healing process, and provides
essential information about the known causes of pre-
birth loss as well as about GP and hospital practices.

Health/Women's Studies £6.99
ISBN 0 7043 4457 2

The Women's Press Handbook Series

Gerrilyn Smith
The Protectors' Handbook
Reducing the Risk of Child Sexual Abuse
and Helping Children Recover

How much more effective would we be in working
against child sexual abuse if every adult had the
knowledge currently available only to professionals?

With child sexual abuse now unquestionably
widespread, every adult in contact with children
must – and can – be an active protector. Now, in this
unique and essential book, child psychologist,
Gerrilyn Smith, gives adults all the information and
skills needed to protect children in their day-to-day
lives. Drawing on her many years of professional
experience in the field, a wide range of sources and
proven techniques – as well as the experiences of
young survivors themselves – she offers a fully
comprehensive, practical and step-by-step guide
to recognising, reducing the risks of and overcoming
the effects of abuse.

From being aware of the many possible signs of abuse
to helping a child confide, from creating the best
context for recovery to finding the most appropriate
professional help, this urgently needed, accessible
book is absolutely essential reading for every adult.

Health/Self Help £6.99
ISBN 0 7043 4417 3

The Women's Press Handbook Series

Margaret Doyle
The A-Z of Non-Sexist Language

Bringing today's vocabulary completely up-to-date,
here is a definitive guide to non-sexist language.

With a complete listing of sexist words and their non-
sexist alternatives; vital clarification of common-usage
words – outlining fully why some words are sexist
and others are not; full cross-referencing; and an
easy-to-use A-Z dictionary format, here is an
invaluable handbook for writers, editors, teachers,
speakers and all who care about the words they use.

Reference/Language £6.99
ISBN 0 7043 4430 0

The Women's Press Handbook Series

Casey Miller and Kate Swift
The Handbook of Non-Sexist Writing
For Writers, Editors and Speakers

Third British Edition – Fully revised and updated

How can we avoid sexist language and find clear and
elegant ways of saying what we mean? In this classic
and definitive handbook, Casey Miller and Kate Swift
offer essential solutions to the use of sexist clichés,
suffixes, prefixes, pronouns, titles, categories and
terms. Now fully revised and updated, here is a lively
and informative companion for any writer, journalist,
teacher, editor and lover of the English language.

**'An essential aid for anyone who makes his or her
living out of words, as well as a sensible guide for
people who know that an even-handed language
would help towards an even-handed world.'**
Cosmopolitan

Reference/Language/Women's Studies £6.99
ISBN 0 7043 4442 4